Still With It!

Still With It!

The Funny Side of Growing Older

Peter Buckman

Illustrations by Jack Dunnington

THE EXPERIMENT

NEW YORK

The Experiment, LLC
220 East 23rd Street, Suite 600
New York, NY 10010-4658
theexperimentpublishing.com

This book contains the opinions and ideas of its author. It is intended to provide
helpful and informative material on the subjects addressed in the book. It is sold
with the understanding that the author and publisher are not engaged in rendering
medical, health, or any other kind of personal professional services in the book.
The author and publisher specifically disclaim all responsibility for any liability,
loss, or risk—personal or otherwise—that is incurred as a consequence, directly or
indirectly, of the use and application of any of the contents of this book.

Many of the designations used by manufacturers and sellers to distinguish their
products are claimed as trademarks. Where those designations appear in this book
and The Experiment was aware of a trademark claim, the designations have been
capitalized.

The Experiment's books are available at special discounts when purchased in bulk
for premiums and sales promotions as well as for fund-raising or educational use. For
details, contact us at info@theexperimentpublishing.com.

Library of Congress Cataloging-in-Publication Data available upon request

ISBN 978-1-61519-596-1
Ebook ISBN 978-1-61519-597-8

Cover and text design and cover illustration by Beth Bugler
Illustrations by Jack Dunnington

Manufactured in China

First printing September 2019
10 9 8 7 6 5 4 3 2 1

For my grandchildren,
Michael and Emma, who have
so much to look forward to.

Author's Note

I am in my late seventies, happily married to the same woman for fifty years, proud parent of two daughters and grandparent of two children who are the most beautiful, intelligent, and creative creatures in the known universe. I've had a reasonably successful career as a publisher and writer, and I'm still working as a literary agent; I'm active and healthy, despite two forms of cancer; we own the house we've lived in for nearly half a century in a beautiful Oxfordshire village; and my only brush with the law, apart from going on demonstrations, was when I was busted for speeding. And yet I need reassurance. Probably we all do. Maybe it's part of our instinctive reactions: When confronted with a threat we freeze, fight, flee—or offer reassurance.

And we wouldn't have lasted this long if our instincts weren't reliable.

But how do you access your instincts when they're encrusted with experience? You get yourself a book that shares the thoughts, exposes the fears, and celebrates at least some of the actions you have hitherto kept to yourself. It's no surprise that the earliest bestsellers were guides to etiquette, sex, and cooking: These are areas of life where we want to give pleasure as well as receive it, and we want to be reassured that we're doing things properly. Yet while there are endless books on how to raise our kids, there are precious few on how to embrace the aging process. Which, considering how many there are of us seniors—so many we're a threat to the Social Security budget—is a little surprising.

We don't think we're old until suddenly we can't do something that until now has never been a problem. We don't feel we're old because our habits and reactions were formed when we were younger, and as they served us well we see no reason to change them. But we're not immune to new ideas, we're always open to persuasion, we retain our curiosity about the latest discovery and our willingness to learn. Don't we? We don't want to be lectured or patronized or told how we should behave by people who don't know what they're talking about—so why should you listen to a white middle-class male who is a Jewish, atheist, vegetarian socialist with anti-monarchy leanings? Because you, like me, want reassurance, too.

There are no prescriptions in this book, which is a personal hodgepodge of snapshot descriptions, opinions, remembrances, suggestions, and the occasional exhortation. If you believe that civility, good manners, and good humor are what keep us going, I hope you will enjoy, recognize, and be reassured by these entries. Incidentally, I've used the words "I," "you," and "we" indiscriminately, assuming we have in common many of the experiences described. If not, I apologize, but I'm afraid there's no money-back guarantee.

Advice should be dispensed only when requested. Of course we know a million times more than the younger generation, otherwise we've wasted an awful lot of years, but even though we're bursting with wisdom that will change everyone's lives for the better, drowning people in it will only make them sputter with indignation. Advice is like chocolate and should be offered sparingly. My father used to say: "Get the best advice you can, then do the opposite." A subversive view, but worth considering.

Age can be a bit of a problem for us seniors: If you tell people how old you are, they'll think you're either lying or fishing for compliments. Or, worse, use it as a cue to launch a list of all the ailments (p. 7) they've endured or overcome on the way to being (probably) a few years younger than *you* are. The thing is, nobody prepares you to behave appropriately for your age, as very few of us feel we're as old as we are. Of course our bodies remind us we can't jump around like we used to, but though we may recognize that we are old, or older, at least in the eyes of the young, few of the virtues we thought would accrue with age have materialized. Do you feel grown-up now that you're past seventy? Of course not. Are you more patient, tolerant, forgiving, and mellow? Yeah, right. When you're stuck behind someone strictly observing the speed limit, do you mutter approvingly? Really? Do you act more responsibly than you did when you were younger? Only if you need to reassure your children and grandchildren. One thing age does is make you a better actor. My mother knew how to deal with age. She would never mention how old she was until she was well into her nineties (and she continued to have her hair dyed a fiery red until after her 100th birthday). One day, a much younger neighbor told her how lovely she looked. She told him he looked lovely, too, to which he replied he could never hope to look as elegant as she did. "How kind," she said. "I suppose I'm not bad for ninety-seven." "Ooh," he countered, "a woman who'll tell you her age will tell you anything." My mother leaned forward conspiratorially. "What would you like to know?" she asked.

Ailments form the list of everything that's wrong with us, with which we regale our friends, unless they get into it first. We naturally feel sympathy for someone who has a crippling, debilitating, or fatal disease, but most of us secretly draw an invisible circle around them and silently give thanks that we aren't similarly affected. We privately tell ourselves that the victim's past behavior—their sexual shenanigans, their smoking and boozing—are probably to blame for their condition, and we make ourselves believe we were far more restrained. Or maybe it's the fault of their genes, for which neither they nor we can be held responsible. Of course, if we suspect we've

got something nasty, we seek medical advice, but those aches and pains we wake up with—or, worse, get up with in the middle of the night—become as familiar as the layout of the room we fumble around on our way to the bathroom in the dark. Tell yourself that click in your knee is just cartilage, not cancer, and it won't stop you going for a walk. Ailments, the minor ones, are just reminders that we should respect the bodies that have served us well, at least so far.

Amateurs used to be the proud pioneers of science and commerce until people calling themselves professionals claimed that a modern society needed specially trained experts to manage matters efficiently. As these same experts have made a complete mess of everything from the economy to the environment, the stock of amateurs—people like us who worked out the best way of doing things for ourselves—has risen somewhat. I'm not saying our views on the exchange rate will be taken any more seriously than our attempts at grouting tiles, but at a time when we are overwhelmed by ignorance and incompetence, we amateurs should retain the courage to speak out and contribute our two cents' worth.

Ambition is something you should cultivate even if you've long ago retired from full-time work and boast—when drunk, depressed, or seeking sympathy— that you've achieved all the goals you once set yourself. Without something to aim for you risk getting bored, and boredom (p. 26) is what kills you. An ambition should be just (but not too far) beyond your reach, and within your grasp if you can grab it without injuring yourself. Now that you're a comfortable age you can rule out being the fastest, richest, best-looking, or most powerful person on the planet, but you can still do your daily walk a bit quicker, or fill in the crossword or sudoku faster, or cook a dish you've never tried before to impress your friends. You can lobby to become chair of the committee you're on, because you know you'd handle it better than the incumbent. You could do things you've never gotten around to, like playing jazz piano or mastering mah-jongg, and once you've acquired the basics you'll play to win because you've never really lost the competitive spirit that keeps you going. You may say you have, but you know yourself better than that. Ambition means looking forward, and that's got to be better than looking back.

Anger can be a wonderful release, but, like all indulgences, it should be saved for special occasions. It's fine to express your irritation at politicians, foreign dictators, writers with whom you violently disagree, overacting thespians, people who stop dead in front of you to jab at their phones, and stupidity in all its forms; but if you succumb to rage with those dear to you, you may feel better, but it will only be temporary. Though we would never admit it publicly, age gnaws away at our previously held conviction that we are always in the right. I waited until I was forty to have a serious shouting match with my father, who was behaving like an ass when we were all on vacation at my parents' house in the South of France, probably because he resented being removed from day-to-day responsibility for the firm he'd founded. Our argument began when he accused me of not helping enough to entertain their guests, and it escalated to the point when I told him we would never again stay with them. At first I felt grown-up, independent, principled, and courageous, but then I began to feel I'd orphaned myself and missed the tight-knit embrace of the family I grew up in, the comfort of customs that are both appealing and appalling. The cause of my anger shrank into insignificance, and it occurred to me that I might have overreacted. We made up when meeting around the hospital bed of my sister, who had just given birth to her first child, and the argument was never again referred to. Anger directed at those who are closest to you may be cathartic, but the changes you hoped your shouting would bring about almost never occur. Maturity brings doubt, and once you start to think you might have acted wrongly, you will suffer insomnia and indigestion until you are reconciled.

Apologies: Sorry, but you're going to have to learn to apologize, and sooner rather than later. My wife maintained that I was incapable of saying "sorry" because I couldn't openly admit I was wrong, but age has changed that, at least a little. Occasionally, and either under unbearable provocation or the influence of drink, you may behave badly toward someone—who is being rude or obnoxious or simply ill-mannered—and if, when the mist has receded, you accept that you acted like an oaf, then, as a reasonable and grown-up person, I am sure you will see the need for an apology. You may offer it grudgingly or generously, and it may or may not be accepted, but at least you've made the gesture, and if they choose to reject it, that's their problem. But it's much harder to apologize for something you've blurted out when you're in an argument, or just a heated discussion, and your back's to the wall. At such moments your tongue leapfrogs your brain and you say something truly hurtful. I'm not talking about insisting on something as fact that later proves to be fiction: Maturity means graciously accepting you may have made a mistake. Much harder to apologize for, and much harder for the abused party to accept, is the hot-tongued insult, the personal criticism that is so wounding because both of you are jolted into wondering if it reflects your true feelings. On such occasions apologies go unheeded, and it can take an astonishingly long time before the abused person is persuaded you really didn't mean it. You can always find excuses for your behavior, such as drink (again), or a combination of frustration and instability caused by stress that resulted in a temporary mental aberration that you deeply regret, but your apology, however heartfelt, will need to be backed by genuinely good behavior for an appreciable period before it will be accepted as sincere. Sorry, but there it is.

Appearance is vitally important because it's what others judge you on. The first impression the eye sends to the brain decides in an instant what someone thinks of you, and however witty or rich or fascinating you are, you're going to have to work really hard to overcome a negative view formed by a run in your tights or snot on your tie. To be free of vanity you have to be a saint or an eccentric, and while it may be virtuous to not care how you look, very few of us look good without a bit of help. Beautiful people, in my experience, rarely accept or acknowledge their special quality—indeed, they often deny it. The rest of us may not aspire to beauty, or be able to rely on natural elegance to face the world with confidence, but the experience and self-knowledge that our years confer means accepting that it takes us a while to get ready properly. Those who enjoy a supportive relationship may let their partner decide which clothes go best together; otherwise you have to check your instincts by looking in the mirror. Some of us become color blind with age, and insist with increasing vehemence that things don't clash when our partner says they do. If you can't find an independent arbitrator—a grandchild won't do, as they shouldn't be dragged into domestic disputes—I suggest you climb down with what grace you can muster. If you're going out together, your partner won't want to be seen with someone who has no sense of style, will they?

Appetite for food, sex, or new experience does
not diminish with age. When good food and wine are
put in front of me, I will carry on eating and drinking
until either I or they are forcibly removed, whereas
my wife can control her impulses, say she is full, and
be strong-minded enough to refuse further helpings.
Our younger daughter, who had eating disorders, has
suggested I leave a little bit on my plate to tell my brain
that I've had enough, but I find I'm incapable of such
self-discipline. I sometimes claim it's because I was
born during the Second World War, when food was
rationed and if I didn't finish everything on my plate I
was reminded, by hungry relatives who had probably
given up some of their ration to ensure I was properly
fed, that the world was full of starving children who
would be glad to have my leftovers. In my formative
years I went to a boys-only school where if you didn't
gulp down everything quickly, someone else would steal
your portion. But I accept that I am greedy and eat too
much too fast because I enjoy it. Of course it leads to
an expanding waistline, and of course I should train
myself to have smaller portions and chew everything
thirty times (which supposedly fools the brain into
thinking you're full, besides making the food easier to
digest), and wait twenty minutes before helping myself

to chocolate, but sadly the only thing that stiffens my resolve is a severe stomachache. Weighing responsibility against temptation, where food is concerned the latter is an easy winner, whereas with sex, at least for an aging male, the parts that connect appetite to action are often so unreliable that temptation can be resisted.

Approval: As a plant needs water, we need approval from our partners, friends, colleagues, people we work with, and people who work for us. Children want their parents' approval, but they don't often realize that their parents want their approval, too, along with their love and respect (we don't ask too much, do we?). Religious zealots want the approval of their god, politicians want the approval of the electorate, and even blood-soaked tyrants want the approval of their supporters, though the latter are terrorized into giving it. The danger for us seniors is that we know from long experience how to gain approval, and we end up doing it from habit rather than conviction. When someone we respect—a friend we haven't seen for a while, or a guru at whose feet we once sat—points out how we have changed and lost our youthful fire, compromising our principles, agreeing with theories we used to attack, or being polite to someone who deserves to be roundly criticized, we are outraged. We will say that life is too short to fight every battle, that being pragmatic is more effective than pacing the windy moral high ground, that we have learned over the years that there are some people whose views we will never change. But of course, if we simply admitted our critic was right, and that all we really wanted was for everyone to like us, they might call us pathetic, but they'd have to approve of our honesty (p. 98).

Arousal can still surprise us, and that's got to be a good thing. An image, a photograph, a body whose owner is proud of the work they've put into it, a dancer or an athlete showing muscular grace, the memory of an ecstatic coupling, the touch of a lover that promises nothing but is freighted with possibility: These things can arouse desire without the obligation of performance. I'm not suggesting we're no longer capable of sexual fulfillment, only that if, as I hope, we all have a full bank of memories, it gives us a generous amount of credit we needn't expend all at once. If pornography (p. 149) is arousal for instant gratification, there is a more thoughtful and subtle form of arousal that sets the wires of experience crackling with energy without the need to come in a neon starburst.

Attitude, like ambition (p. 9), is an essential attribute for an active senior, for it defines us. If you don't keep up with current developments and take a view on them, people (especially the young) will think you don't know or don't care about things that matter to them, and they will consider you out of touch, which is an insult to your knowledge and intelligence. Adopt a listening pose and it gives you license to expound. Once you get going you can be opinionated, provided you restrain yourself from pointing out how little they know. Even if you don't win the argument or make any converts, if you can articulate your attitude you stand a reasonable chance of being taken seriously.

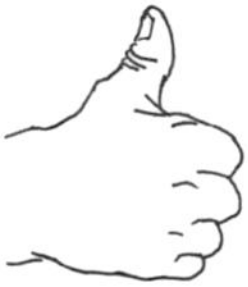

B

Bad behavior is our way of showing that we can still shock, surprise, and kick against what others expect of us, but we know, and have always known, the difference between that and behavior that is criminal. In our youth we may have tried shoplifting to gain acceptance by a gang, but that didn't lead to a career in burglary any more than a drunken fumble led to rape: We understood the meaning of the word *no*, even if we also knew of sexist pigs who abused their power and position to commit criminal acts. You don't forget the difference between right and wrong when you grow old, and it would be a tragedy if we let others' crimes stop us from being provocative, outrageous, flirtatious, or rude when the occasion demands it. That way blandness lies.

Beauty can be described as an arrangement of features, whether natural or contrived—in a face, a body, a landscape, a painting, a piece of writing or music—that stirs up an instinctive sense of appreciation. The effect is not something you think about; it simply happens, though of course different things affect different people in different ways. I find beauty in a sunlit field, you might find it in a mountainous crag that would give me vertigo, but what matters is what, if anything, we do about it. Beauty ought to be celebrated when there is so much ugliness around, but gallantry can be mistaken for predation, and wisdom dictates that you limit your compliments to those you know will appreciate them.

Bereavement is something nobody can prepare for. My mother died at 103 but it took me a long while to feel the sadness that seemed appropriate—indeed, when people called to express their condolences, I felt I was letting them down by not grieving as much as they expected. Doubtless that's because my mother went through a long decline, and her death was a relief to her and to her children, but though I miss her I only cried for her when mourning the death of a friend's daughter. When my father died, suddenly and unexpectedly, at eighty-one, I tried and failed to squeeze some tears out, but they didn't flow naturally until several months later, when I saw a Chinese film that must have reminded me of his passion for that country, and perhaps the combination of memory, love, and bereavement led me to sob bitterly all the way home.

Crying, of course, is an emotional reaction over which we have little control, like that rapidly suppressed flash of glee that bubbles up when you hear of a death, not because you're glad someone's gone but because you're relieved to still be around. You'd think that at our age we'd have had enough experience to know how to cope with death. And you'd be wrong, because you can never tell how it will take you.

Of course, the death of a child, or the person you've been loving and living with for many joyful years, is such an appalling prospect you can't armor yourself against it. The mature reaction to such a loss is not to pretend you know how to deal with it but to wait until it happens and then cope with as much dignity as you can muster. Some analysts say a child is mature only when it accepts that its parents will eventually die. Now we are all living for so much longer, maybe our children will be relieved as well as saddened by our deaths, as I was at my mother's. So to hell with behaving as other people expect when mourning: Let's go with our instincts, whether they involve snot or stoicism, and trust that when it's our turn we, too, will be properly missed, however people choose to show it.

Betrayal: We, of course, would never betray a confidence, let alone someone we loved—though sometimes I have let slip a tiny secret (p. 172), unimportant and unlikely to cause harm because it would have come out anyway, and besides I was among friends and had taken a glass or two and simply forgot that I was supposed to keep it to myself. Which is totally different from, say, being tortured by nasty people to reveal details of an operation with which I might have some vague connection; not being heroic enough to withstand pain, of course I'd tell them whatever they wanted to hear.

Sometimes, however, people of our generation are betrayed by someone close—a partner, a lover, even a spouse. We hope we have reached the stage when our serious relationships are not only stable but taking us together through waters that, despite an occasional storm, are relatively calm, certainly compared to our earlier years. And then something happens that is totally unexpected and devastating, the sort of thing you read about—Wife Leaves Husband for Childhood Sweetheart After Forty Years of Marriage"—and it's a betrayal so immense and so humiliating no one will believe you when you say you never saw it coming. Adultery is a betrayal of a relationship, and comes from the same root as corrupting or diluting something. When a friend suffered from this catastrophe, we all rallied around him, and were soon introducing him to new people as though he were divorced or widowed. The trouble was, he couldn't believe he had been guilty of doing anything that provoked the betrayal, whether it was some casual infidelity that had come to light, or some act of selfishness that had led to festering resentment. Eventually he found someone else, but we were concerned that if he'd learned nothing from the experience, it might be repeated. Betrayal blows up your very foundations, and as you can't build on rubble, you have to dig deep to create something new.

Birthdays are occasions I take very seriously.

I know many prefer to avoid commemorating the
passing of the years, as merely reciting the numerals
makes them feel ancient. For me, they are an
opportunity to celebrate being
alive despite occasional illness,
frequent disappointment,
periodic frustration, and
my inability to persuade
people that a civilized polity
is possible if only they were sensible and shared my
beliefs. In a good year, birthdays offer proof that
despite being an age I would once have regarded
as totally decrepit, I don't entirely look it, and can
certainly behave childishly. I love surprises (they
keep you on your toes) and my family knows that and
generously surprises me. And, of course, birthdays
are an opportunity to be generous in a personal and
thoughtful way. It's not the gifts—the older we get,
the less clutter most of us want—it's the act of making
contact, choosing a card, organizing a gathering,
toasting survival. Birthdays are individual occasions,
free from the commercialization of high holidays
like Christmas or manufactured obligations like
Mother's Day. I like to celebrate mine at least three

times—once in anticipation, once on the actual day, once to postpone the feeling it's all over and may never be repeated. Far from keeping our birthdays quiet, I think we should enjoy them as vigorous proof of our continuing presence, being generous to our friends and enjoying the annoyance of our enemies.

Book groups are a form of social intercourse that can be intellectually stimulating, while being (usually) less competitive than game nights. You get to see other people's houses, maybe drink their wine and nibble their canapés, meet new people, diplomatically criticize their taste (at least in books), and read something you would never normally pick up. Most members are women, and their literary interests are usually more adventurous than men's—one group I know read all three volumes of Fifty Shades of Grey while their male partners concentrated on a history of the Peninsular War. On the other hand, when it's your turn to act as host you have to clean to exceptional standards, prepare (or buy) morsels that are dainty and distinctive without making you look like a show-off, and offer wine better than you would normally imbibe. And then you have to think of a book for everyone to read next time, which involves a great deal of research,

in addition to having intelligent comments to make about the work you're there to discuss, which you've hardly had time to look at, given all the other burdens of hospitality. Also, over time the other members' views can become predictable, they interrupt just when you're developing a point or, worse, they say what you were going to say before you can articulate it. And though everyone is a volunteer, forcing yourself to read a new book every month somehow smacks of being made to do your homework, with virtue often being eclipsed by resentment. But then, what other than a book can get you out of the house, charge up your brain, and lead you to encounter new faces, new ideas, and new writers?

Boredom can be fatal. Being a wage slave may have been boring, but that was the tedium of the routine. Hopefully the work had some point, and at least you were regularly rewarded. Boredom is when you don't have the mental energy to set yourself goals or follow a routine that gets you nearer to achieving them. It's like being ill: You can't operate at full throttle; you mope around until you feel better, but you'll never feel better if at the end of the day you've got nothing to show for your suffering. It isn't having nothing to do—that problem can be solved with drink or other distractions. It's having nothing to do that seems enjoyable or worthwhile. Mowing the lawn is boring, but the result is pleasing, so the effort pays off. You can spend days trying to build or decorate or even compose something that doesn't come right away, but you persevere because you get a kick out of it, or at least learn from the experience. Boredom is when nothing seems inviting, enticing, or engaging; when you've lost control of your imagination and ambition and feel like giving up. Like depression (p. 53) and other debilitating states of mind, you have to realize what's happening and make the decision to change it. Nobody else can do it for you.

C

Calories should, we are frequently told, be counted religiously if we want to keep fit and avoid obesity. Which is fine if you like making lists (p. 116) and you're obsessive about weighing your portion of breakfast oats and consulting your guide so that you can give yourself the joyous news that you've got 1,894 calories left for the rest of your day—but can you rely on the guide's accuracy? We've lived through enough changes of "expert opinion" to be mistrustful. If eggs are bad for you one week and good for you the next, can we be confident that the number of calories they supposedly contain is scientifically precise? Of course we all cheat a little on our own, "forgetting" to count that tiny bit of butter that would otherwise go to waste, splashing a bit more gin into our glass that takes it over the "standard" measure, but how were those figures printed in bold on labels arrived at? When car manufacturers cheat on their emission and consumption figures, are food and drink manufacturers immune? Just worrying about this question probably uses as many calories as a brisk walk, because the brain expends an amazing amount of energy, but who adds that to the reckoning? Let's face it, if you're going to obsess about your calories, it's best to embrace your competitive side and join a fitness group, because doing it on your own is (a) ineffectual, as you're bound to lose patience and cheat, and (b) rather sad.

Caution creeps up on you. We've all learned, over the years, to be cautious about things like weather or economic forecasts, the opinions of so-called experts, members of the opposite sex who insist they want a no-strings relationship, and anyone who offers the investment of a lifetime. But there's a difference between being cautious about advice and cautious about action. Say someone proposes you accompany them on an adventure vacation in a place you've never

visited. When you were young you would have accepted
without a second thought, right? Now, you weigh up
the disadvantages—the cost, the tedium of getting
there, the dangers and discomfort of roughing it in a
place unprepared for tourism, the amount of pills and
potions you'll have to pack, and the risk of running out
of essential supplies—and you think, fuck it, I'd rather
stay at home. On the one hand you are conserving your
resources and will probably live longer by avoiding
bandits and mysterious infections, on the other you are
depriving yourself of an experience that could enhance
your life with a jolt of the unusual. Being sensible
about taking risks is one thing, being cautious about
the unexpected may verge on cowardice (p. 43). It's the
perennial conflict between instinct and intellect that we
all have to face, with one consolation: If we err on the
side of caution, at our age we are used to living with
regret (p. 161).

Celebrations of an old friend's life, whether
they're living or dead, are like that extra bit of
chocolate: You grab at it greedily, knowing you'll
probably regret it afterward. You accept an invitation
to a memorial because you want to pay tribute
and comfort the family, and also because you want

privately to celebrate your own survival and see how you compare to those contemporaries who are left. But when you've schlepped yourself over to wherever the event is taking place, complaining at the cost and difficulty of getting there when you'd be much more comfortable at home, where your own wine is far superior to that served at the party, and knowing there'll never be enough food worth eating, you encounter all the problems involved in facing up to your past. People look vaguely familiar but you can't remember their names and think it's rude to ask. When you introduce yourself they can't hear you, so you have to shout; they look blank, but announce their own name, which you can't quite catch. If you do find someone you know, you quickly discover there's very little to talk about once you've lied about them not having changed, and exchanged lists of ailments (p. 7). If it's a large party, the noise is deafening, the speeches inaudible, and you wonder who all these young people are who couldn't possibly have known your aged friend, and while some of them may talk politely to you, they have no idea of your reputation and probably are only there for the booze. Old acquaintances seem to have become bent and boring, never mind losing their sense of humor: Either they don't appreciate your attempt to add levity to the proceedings by making witty comments, or they're too deaf or drunk to care. The opportunity such events offer of catching up with people you once held dear can be hollow and disappointing—but of course you will go on attending them while you can, if only to show you're still around.

Celebrity is a sunbeam of recognition from gods we don't believe in. When I was young, I told myself that the thrill I got from talking to somebody famous was because they had achieved something that was beyond the reach of ordinary people, even those (like me and you) with unlimited ambition. There was a reason they had achieved celebrity status: They were the best at what they did, supreme at the summit of the mountains the rest of us were waiting to climb. Now we are more experienced, and perhaps a touch embittered after getting a little lost on our way to the top, we can be grateful at not being celebrities, and be at ease in their company. When once we mocked their desire for privacy, and told ourselves we could cope with the scalding heat of fame as long it was accompanied by a reasonable fortune and the ability to get a table in fashionable restaurants, now we mock their frequently chronicled failings, pity their inability to sustain lasting relationships, agree with those who ascribe their success to chance or corruption or clever marketing rather than talent, and unworthily rejoice when their reputations are shredded. We'd still have dinner with them, though. A fallen angel still has wings.

Chance and luck (p. 119) are different, in my opinion. Chance begins a process, luck plays a part in completing or defeating it. You can't rely on chance, but you can make your own luck: Chance may afflict you with an awful disease, luck—and getting the right medical attention—may see you cured. Experienced people like us should be able to recognize luck, in the sense of it being an opportunity, but only a wild optimist, bordering on fantasist, would count on being rescued by chance in the sense of the random operation of forces beyond our understanding. The trouble is few of us learn from our own mistakes, let alone other people's, and we persist in confusing the various meanings of chance in the hope of getting out of trouble. We welcome a chance meeting that leads to new opportunities as a sign of fate being on our side; if it all goes wrong, even the most mature of us is apt to deny responsibility and blame factors outside our control. We all know, and tell others, that things shouldn't be left to chance, but that doesn't stop us doing just that. It's a sign of our gambling nature, and possibly our laziness, but assuming we've avoided plunging our families into destitution, we will doubtless continue to avoid practicing what we preach.

Change is difficult and uncomfortable, but that doesn't mean we should avoid it. It can be forced on us by unexpected circumstances: an accident, an illness, or a malfunction in a machine we rely on, such as a car or computer. If your partner suddenly breaks a leg and needs you to abandon your usual activities to take care of them, you're going to show what an adaptable, tolerant, responsible person you are, and change accordingly. The odd thing is, the older we get the more we grumble about change, yet we often face the greatest change of all, from independence to dependence, with little or no preparation. I suppose it's because it's something we don't want to think about too much, as we're secretly confident we'll cope when we have to. Like always.

Charity can be immensely satisfying if you're working for one or supporting a worthy (and effective) organization with your philanthropic donations, but it can consume you with guilt when you don't have much money and are deluged with requests for help. One elderly woman killed herself because she couldn't cope with the sheer volume of competing demands from good causes, but that shouldn't stop us from giving altogether. Charity contributes to our well-being: It allows most of us to feel better about ourselves for a relatively small outlay and very little effort. When you see pictures of individual victims of war, famine, natural disaster, birth defects, epidemics, or simple poverty, your instinct is to offer them money. You know that some of it will be siphoned off by corrupt officials, that the aid it buys will be exploited by criminals, and anyway won't be nearly enough to help all those in need, but even so it's better than doing nothing. Charity is a poor way of righting the wrongs of the world, but the victims deserve our support, as do the people who work for them, if only because there is little chance we'd go out and do what they're doing.

Children: You knew you were doing something right when your children moaned at you for being so restrictive, and your parents gently (but pointedly) criticized you for letting your offspring run wild. Now that we are grandparents we can spoil our grandchildren with impunity, but how do we develop a relationship with our offspring that is supportive, tolerant, and resilient enough to withstand the inevitable fights? Especially when they move back in with us because they can't afford a place of their own, or they've lost their job, or broken up with a partner and have nowhere else to go. We're glad to see them, of course, and for a while their presence makes a welcome change. But when the new routines (p. 169) we have established as empty nesters are interrupted or disregarded, and the spaces we have taken over are suddenly occupied, while we love our children and are full of sympathy for their predicament, it's hard to avoid just a touch of resentment and frustration at the way we're being used. Doubtless they feel the same.

Our generation prides itself on having a very different, and much warmer, relationship with our own children than our parents had with us. We set boundaries for our kids to bounce off, we tried not to make threats that we couldn't or wouldn't carry out, but perhaps the biggest difference was that we explained the reasons for the rules we wanted them to observe, rather than simply laying them down. My childhood relationship with my parents was based on me accepting their authority; my relationship with my children was

based on justifying whatever authority I wielded. If we
can move on from the fact that our parents' behavior
toward us was irritating, unfair, and often irrational and
accept that they were far from perfect but convinced
they were doing their best, we should try and persuade
our own children to see us, too, as loving but flawed.
When they're young, children want their parents to be
infallible; by the time they're teenagers they know we
often make mistakes; when they're adults we must hope
the mistakes they may have made help them to regard
us more tolerantly, especially if they're sharing our
space. Closeness means you can confront your problems
together, which is some compensation for the strain
caused by enforced proximity.

Chores are jobs you want to get out of the way so
you can do something more creative, but they can also
give you a sense of achievement. None of us wants
them to define our day: We have moved on from the
time when routine tasks, such as the housework that was
expected of women when we were young, are considered
fulfilling in themselves. Now that we have reached the
age when we don't have to clock in to work or answer to
bosses or do jobs we know are beneath or beyond us, we
are entitled to take a break and do little or nothing once

we've laid the table, sorted out the fire or boiler, and dealt with the washing. The trouble is that doing little or nothing soon strengthens the acid of Puritan guilt (p. 89). We bring in the firewood or get the ironing out of the way, and then what? Why are we in such a hurry to be done with the chores when we haven't decided, or simply don't know, what to do with the rest of our time? Shouldn't we take things more slowly, to allow further plans to develop and mature? There are those who say the urge to deal with little matters quickly is a product of the internet culture, and particularly the pressure to respond instantly to emails. But it surely goes back to the time when the provider was forced to stand aside for somebody younger, and invented a list of tasks to keep themselves occupied and make them seem indispensable. We're always in a rush because we don't know what's around the corner, but if there really isn't something you're desperate to do once you've taken out the trash, remember that the more chores you do, the more chores there will be for you to do, and take your time.

Competing might be an evolutionary thing to ensure we survive as a species, but you would have thought that when we've reached the age of watching our grandchildren grow up, we'd stop worrying about whether our car will look as good as those of the other people collecting them from school, or whether our clothes are the right mix of hip and casual without looking flashy or dowdy. We carry on competing in ways that can be subtle ("Oh, you still go to the store? I buy everything online") and crude ("I wouldn't be seen dead in one of those bargain supermarkets; their wines are so hit-and-miss"). It seems we can't stop ourselves competing against each other, even though our place in the pecking order has long been established. Either it's a habit we can't kick, or a way of proving we still have a kick in us, that no one can take us for granted. Competing is perfectly healthy provided you don't let it become a consuming and destructive lust for a victory that is beyond your financial or physical grasp; and providing that you limit the competition to people of your own age and situation. The young will find you competing against them laughable, and everyone will find you competing against easy targets contemptible.

Confidence seems to become more brittle as you grow older. It would be nice to think that we keep it polished like a favorite pair of shoes, so that it's flexible and resistant to stains, but often an unexpected knock puts a big hole in it. Experience should make us resilient, but it doesn't matter whether you're a politician or a poet, criticism hurts and confidence suffers. We tell ourselves we should be grown-up about it and not let ourselves be affected, but what sensitive person like you or me doesn't think there might be some truth in what our critics are saying? It's taken me years to be confident that the way I think and feel is shared by enough people to justify me writing a book like this, but I hope I'm confident enough to listen to differing views, for ignoring them would be a sign of insensitivity and inflexibility. Mind you, only a saint or a tyrant maintains their confidence in the face of fierce opposition: Myself, I need a good sulk and a stiff drink before my confidence levels trickle back to normal.

Conscience may soften with age, like almost everything else, but there's a thin steel core that is both flexible and indestructible. Years of using and abusing the moral code we call conscience teaches us what we can get away with, but as with bad behavior (p. 19) however much we have compromised there are still some basic things we don't do (unless we're totally depraved). Conscience is what keeps us civilized, makes us predictable to our children, acceptable to our partners, and reliable to our friends. Far from making you a moralizing bore, it's actually something to boast of and celebrate, like having your own hair and teeth.

Cooking contributes hugely to my well-being. I'm not particularly good at it, and I promise I'm not going to give you my favorite recipes, but I started to explore cooking when I became a vegetarian in my early forties, and in my late seventies I've found it embodies almost all the qualities that make our lives enjoyable. You can be spontaneous, inventive, even thrifty when using up food that would otherwise get thrown out. You can follow a recipe, improve on it (or ruin it), or improvise: It's the perfect occupation for the amateur and gifted dilettante (p. 54). Your work has a purpose and isn't just a chore (p. 38); its aim is to satisfy your own appetites and, if cooking for others, to give pleasure (p. 147) and show off your expertise. You can go looking for particular ingredients or you can produce stuff you've actually grown. You can use the latest fancy equipment or make a virtue of simple tools; you can create a huge pile of dishes or gain enormous credit by clearing up as you go. You can take as much time as you need and no one will accuse you of wasting it. Cooking engages the brain, and requires a wide variety of discrete physical and intellectual skills, such as measuring, timing, chopping and slicing, mixing ingredients for anything from pastry to a roux, seasoning, and tasting. It also involves a reasonable amount of exercise, and can legitimately be accompanied, and often improved, by alcohol. You can be as creative as you're capable of being, and if it all goes wrong you will get sympathy rather than censure. What's not to like?

Cowardice is something you redefine as you grow older. It's different from caution (p. 30): When we were young, to be cautious was a sign of sagacity, whereas to be called a coward was the greatest insult. But after decades of learning what we can and can't cope with, it doesn't seem cowardly to avoid involvement in contests we can't win, it's only putting our experience to sensible use. If, like me, you were bullied at school, you felt like a coward for not standing up for yourself, even if no one named you as such. Having weathered the experience, and hopefully learned how to deal with similar situations in adult life, I no longer think of myself as a cowardly boy, just a survivor. Conscientious objectors in the First World War were called cowards, but eventually came to be seen as men of courage and principle. While we would all hope to protect ourselves or our families if we came under attack, avoiding heroics and pointless posturing is a sign of maturity. If gangs of macho youths are squaring up for a fight, you don't step between them, you call the police. If some drunk taunts you, you don't retaliate, you ignore them. We have all suffered humiliations, and with luck they have taught us when to retreat and when to fight back, when to negotiate and when to compromise.

I think that for grown-ups, cowardice isn't running away from what others threaten to do to you; it's refusing to accept responsibility (p. 165) for your own actions. A small example: I was at a party given by an architect friend with a fiery wife. I saw him in close, and doubtless innocent, conversation with another woman in an adjoining room. For some drunken reason, in that mischievous, mildly malicious spirit that enjoys provoking confrontation between contented couples, I told his wife what he was up to. She marched in, smashed his guitar over his head, and marched out again. He was understandably puzzled and asked me what had provoked such an attack. Instead of telling him that I had caused it, I said I had no idea. I felt like a coward, and I still do.

Curiosity can be life enhancing when handled with the delicacy we have acquired over the years. Showing a friendly interest in a complete stranger—a shop assistant or a new bartender in your local bar—and encouraging them to talk about themselves, which everyone enjoys doing, melts their professionalism into something quite friendly, once they're confident you're not a police officer, but merely (in my case) a Harmless Old Fellow. People can surprise you and confound your expectations. I asked a guy in a phone shop about the elegant Chinese calligraphy tattooed on his arm, and he revealed it was his birth sign, a present from someone he was no longer speaking to, and to avoid negative thoughts he was going to have it covered by another tattoo, rather than having it removed. An entire life story in a brief exchange that made me feel better about humanity in general and the young in particular.

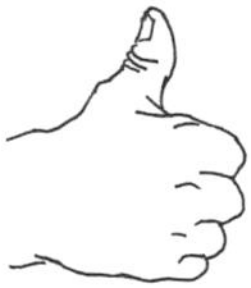

Dancing is an activity our generation is supposed
to be good at. Sadly I'm not, even though I wrote a
social history of dance, which was mainly popular
because of the illustrations. At a ninetieth birthday
party I attended recently, line dancing provided the
entertainment, and oldies not only outnumbered
the youngsters, but outperformed them in technique
and refinement. Even though I'm uncooperative
about doing exactly what everyone else is doing,
their energy and enjoyment was evident. Of course,
dancing is marvelous exercise as well as being a social

grace, and while we can get away with
dancing badly and making a joke of it, if
you've got rhythm you can still learn a few
moves that will surprise and astound your
partner and turn the joke on your friends,
which at our age has to be worth the effort.

Deafness comes to us all, whether
or not we admit it. At first you blame mumbling,
then people talking more softly or less clearly or in
impenetrable accents. You find you're saying "What?"
a lot, in increasingly belligerent tones, as if it were
other people's fault; you turn up the TV and no longer
complain that the music's too loud in movie theaters.
Conversation in bars or at parties becomes difficult,
and you blame the background noise that previously
was never a problem. Your partner or your children
find it funny that you should mishear what they say;
you find it irritating, and also a little alarming, as it's
an unmistakable sign of getting old. For some reason,
nobody (except very young girls) minds wearing glasses,
yet wearing a hearing aid is a badge of shame, as well
as wounding to the vanity. This is partly because of
our memories of bellowing at aged relatives, which
rapidly became boring and tiring. Conversational

gems disintegrate at high volume, which may explain why people at family gatherings would rather spend time with the blind than the deaf. But another reason nobody—or at least nobody I've met—likes hearing aids is because of their design and quality. They may be small and clever and easily hidden by hair, but anyone with half an eye will soon spot the tubes or wires or plug, and the person who's wearing them will give themselves away by turning toward the talker in a marked way that hearing people don't. Regardless of how much you pay, and how invisible the expensive ones claim to be, a hearing aid is still something you stick into an orifice that was designed to repel intruders. Your ear waxes up, the little hairs that sense the sound waves get flattened, voices and (especially) music are distorted. You may be able to hear birdsong again, but until your brain gets used to the increase in volume, crumpling a sheet of paper is as deafening as a tank thundering by. Worst of all is the din inside your head: Chewing food drowns out everything else, and because you believe your voice sounds so loud, you speak much more softly than normally, and people think there's something (else) wrong with you. New hearing aids are more of an irritant than a relief, and what's more they often emit a telltale squeak of feedback when you give someone a hug or a kiss. I find it best to be upfront about it, in the hope people will sympathize rather than regard me as infirm. But let's face it: Deafness is an infirmity, and one that's peculiarly hard to bear.

The **death** of other people is dealt with under *Bereavement,* but our own deserves a separate entry. We all say we don't want to go on forever, and shudder at the thought of losing our marbles (*see Dementia*) or becoming helplessly dependent and confined to bed or wheelchair with little but daytime TV for company. We know that dying is not always a tidy, painless, and dignified process, despite the advances of modern medicine: We may have watched with horror as friends or relatives shrivel in front of us and lose control of their bodies or minds, and though we tell ourselves we won't get like that, we blithely inform our spouse or family they can shoot us if we do, knowing they wouldn't even if they were forced to spend some of their inheritance on paying for our care. On the other hand, if you're suddenly scared into confronting your own mortality—as I was when convinced I had a potentially fatal tumor—your reactions waver from panic and self-pity to anger and disbelief. One moment I wanted to get everything organized so my family wouldn't be left in chaos, the next I wanted to detach myself from the mundane and see the world from an altogether loftier perspective. But of course, when I discovered that the cause of my panic was merely hemorrhoids, my relief washed away my resolve and I behaved much as I did before. Just as when you're feeling well you don't have the courage, the imagination, or the inclination to think about what it's like to be ill, when you watch others dying you convince yourself your own death will be different—your last big surprise. Which is fine, as long as you still enjoy surprises.

Dementia is terrifying because it's so common, so cruel, so random, and—so far—incurable. Everyone knows someone with cancer, which affects one in three of us (it's rising to one in two), but that's a "proper" disease whose symptoms can be scientifically diagnosed, and for which there are treatments that are increasingly successful. You know where you are with a cancer patient: You can talk to them rationally when you visit, discuss their progress, and joke about how much thicker their hair will be when it grows back. But someone suffering from dementia looks exactly as they always have, is probably as fit as they usually are, but the reasoning part of their brain is full of holes. Their actions and reactions are unpredictable, and their partner or caregiver can never be certain of how they will behave. The routines that make everyday life tick along have been exploded. It's as if the victim has left their partner, but their partner cannot leave them. Sometimes they appear lost and bewildered, as ignorant as a baby about who you are and what's going on, though infuriatingly articulate in repeatedly asking the same questions. Sometimes they are abusive, and you never know if they are expressing feelings they have suppressed for years, or merely babbling. There are periods when you think they are happy, or at least contented, in the world that has consumed them, but suddenly their mood will change to one of pathos or anger. It's a truly horrible condition, and though there is some promising research that may help to slow its progress, the number of sufferers is rising. And as we're all hypochondriacs to a greater or lesser extent, we all think that our failure to remember a word or a face or pursue a thought to its conclusion is a sign of impending dementia. Usually it isn't, but that panic gives you an inkling of what the victims endure.

Depression is something I've never suffered from, but it afflicts many people I love. It seems to happen when even the victim least expects it, often not during a crisis but after it has subsided, which is as mystifying to the depressed person as to those around them. The victim withdraws into a cocoon composed more of indifference than self-pity, and is lethargic, remote, and emotionally isolated. I know what is required is patience, sympathy, and a hug if requested, and that the one thing to avoid saying is "Pull yourself together." But though it's an illness it's not like you're dealing with an invalid: Neither of you knows how long the condition will last, and your loving support may go unacknowledged and unappreciated. Depression is no respecter of age, and when it lifts it can leave the sufferer as exhausted as their loved ones. The fact that it's no one's fault consoles nobody, nor does it offer protection against further attacks, though it may be some comfort to tell yourself that these, too, will pass. *See also Moods.*

Dieting is a matter of life and death when you're young, vanity when you're middle-aged, and habit when you're older. The trouble is the older you get, the less difference dieting seems to make. So why do we bother? Partly to show we're in control, partly to demonstrate a degree of well-being (though if you lose a lot of weight, people will ask if you're ill), and partly because we don't want to go to the expense of buying yet larger clothes. That we still care about how we look is a sign of our eternal optimism (p. 136), but it's also worth remembering that medical science says you don't want to be too skinny when you enter your eighties, because you won't cope as well as those who enjoy their food and drink. In moderation, of course.

Dilettantes are people like me who know a little about a lot. I can bullshit with the best on remarkably little research, and as you grow older, provided you keep yourself reasonably well informed and your memory is functional, it's amazing what you can pluck out of a motley collection of facts. Experience gives you an air of authority, and as long as you never claim to be an expert when there's a real one around, a dilettante with charm and chutzpah will be more persuasive than someone who bores on and on about their pet subject.

Disappointment at the way others treat us
is so common we learn to greet it with a brave shrug.
Disappointment with our own failures is harder to
bear. I wanted to write books and scripts that would
change the world and enrich people with the passion
of my arguments and truthfulness of my perceptions,
and here I am writing—with passion and honesty, of
course—about deafness and farting. I mingled with
writers who were bestselling celebrities and told myself
I was at least as good as, if not better than they were,
only lacking their luck and timing. It took me years to
accept that my achievements, though solid, fell some
way short of my youthful ambitions, but acceptance is
a powerful antidote to disappointment. As an oyster
covers an irritating piece of grit with layers of protective
mother-of-pearl, the grit of disappointment can be
layered with realism to produce a pearl. The distance
of years and the satisfaction of survival when others'
successes have been forgotten can also provide the pearl
with a comforting sheen.

Divorce affects more than half of all marriages,
and is surprisingly common among the over-sixties.
For people who've been barely putting up with each
other for years, I can see the appeal in breaking away

and starting a new life while you still have the energy
and enthusiasm for doing things your way instead
of making endless compromises that please neither
party. It must be better to be on your own than in
a relationship that absorbs all your energy without
giving out light or warmth. Some of our generation
divorce and immediately find another partner, with
all the baggage that entails; some are strong enough
to find freedom flying solo. The worst thing about
divorce, apart from its effect on your (hopefully grown-
up) children, and your finances, is what it does to
your circle of friends, who seem to divide along tribal
lines. But then divorce is rarely a spur-of-the-moment
emotional gesture; it involves lawyers and accountants
and argument over the most trivial details. If you can
get through all that and start afresh, the people who
don't understand your travails may not be worth your
friendship anyway.

DIY is something that can be safely left to the
younger generation, who love the opportunity to
show how much more competent they are than
us fumbling duffers. Of course, if you enjoy fixing
things, you should give it a go, provided you're not
a danger to yourself, your family, or your property:

It's easy to persuade yourself you could do as well as the cowboys who masquerade as tradespeople and charge outrageously. But in my experience—and I am neither patient nor good with my hands—anything to do with water, electricity, or load-bearing walls requires a professional, unless you welcome the risk of being ridiculed and having to move to temporary accommodations. *See also Amateurs.*

Dribbling is off-putting in others but excusable when we do it, because of course it's accidental. A sneeze, a snort of laughter, and falling asleep while watching TV can all result in a small effusion, but that's very different from the involuntary dribbling of people who aren't in control of their internal passages. When that happens—and it might, even to us—preventative measures can be taken, whether hankies for the nasal drip or incontinence pads for the lower regions (widely available for men and women, according to Google). I'm not going to say it's nothing to be ashamed of, because losing control is never something to boast about, but as no amount of pelvic floor exercise is going to stop your bladder eventually letting you down, and there is no equivalent exercise for your nose, you might as well accept the fact that

you're going to have to spend more on absorbent materials. If you don't, you'll start to smell as the damp patches dry or the white crusty stuff settles in your jowls, and you really don't want to turn into someone nobody wants to visit, let alone sit next to at a party.

Drink is a far more sociable relaxant than drugs (p. 59), in my opinion, as well as being easily obtainable in a bewildering variety of forms. (I'm talking about alcohol, not water, which we rarely drank for pleasure in my youth. Now young people take water everywhere with them, in case they get dehydrated crossing the road . . . as long as the bottles are recyclable.) Alcohol helps you externalize your thoughts and feelings, unlike drugs, which internalize your experience. Booze makes you relaxed and expansively articulate, at least until that unpredictable tipping point at which sagacity becomes silliness and tolerance turns to intransigence. Unfortunately, our long experience of drink has never taught us when we've had enough, and of course we won't do anything about curbing our drinking until we are forced to.

D

Drugs of the recreational variety aren't a central part of our generation's culture, possibly because when it comes to popping pills our time is taken up with those we've been prescribed. Marijuana, which we called pot or dope or weed, was the drug of choice in our youth, just as cocaine was widely available to our parents' generation. Pot was wasted on me as it put me to sleep—which might have been caused by the tedium of stoned people's conversation, consisting mainly of the word *wow* uttered in a variety of tones—and I only had a toke when it was passed around because it would have been unpardonably square not to do so. There were various pills, uppers and downers, magic mushrooms, and LSD, none of which I tried because I found the sixties quite stimulating enough without chemicals. Nor do I know many of my generation who still take recreational drugs, apart from those who smoke pot for their arthritis. I don't think this is because we've become all moralistic about the damage they can do, though anyone who knows an addict is painfully aware of how difficult it is to deal with their problems. It's more a matter of slowing the pace: Who needs the hectic ups and downs drugs give you when you can spend your money on something you can quietly, and legally (in most states, anyway), enjoy with your friends?

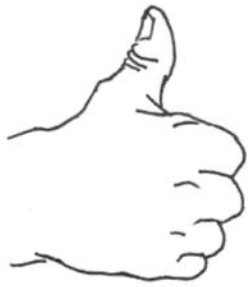

E

Eccentricity should be distinguished from mere affectation. Everyone loves an eccentric, but they are born, not made. The true eccentric is indifferent to what other people feel about them: Their behavior and appearance are natural, not cultivated, even if they are on the just acceptable side of bonkers. It's not eccentric to break out after decades of conformity at work or being in a stifling relationship—it may well be a necessity, and all the more effective for being out of character. Behaving differently—giving vent to a foul-mouthed critical outburst when you're normally mild mannered and agreeable—can completely alter the way people think about you, which can be a good thing if you surprised yourself as much as you surprised them. None of us should be afraid to stand out, but making a habit of it quickly becomes predictable.

Education is about learning stuff, as well as drawing out your talents. Our generation was force-fed facts, and though we may not remember many of them, it still seems that we know a hell of a lot more than our children, let alone our grandchildren. But let's remember that they understand the internet, where all the world's wisdom (and an enormous amount of dubious facts and opinions) is readily available. And they know how to get onto the sites that give them the information they need, whereas we tend to treat computers with a mixture of fear and scorn, to cover the fact that we're afraid we might break something. But one thing's for sure: The advent of artificial intelligence, and the automation of much routine work, means that education is going to have to change from the fixed ladder up, which we trudged, from elementary to middle to high school to college, to a far more flexible system that encourages inventiveness and innovation. It might even resemble our own attempts to extend our horizons now that we are freed from routine toil. Adult education courses tend to be tailored to the needs and abilities of the individual pupil, who is encouraged to learn in a variety of ways from a variety of people for a variety of reasons, from acquiring new qualifications to the sheer pleasure of stimulating the brain. The way our generation continues to learn, choosing what interests us and pursuing it at our own pace, could actually become the norm for those who come after us.

Embarrassing your children is fine as long as you stop short of malice or public humiliation. Embarrassing your grandchildren is what they expect, and they love it because they don't know any better. Embarrassing your family or friends is unforgivable but sadly frequent, especially when drink has been taken. *See also Apologies.*

Encouragement should be ladled out with a lavish hand, unlike advice (p. 5). A parent can be critical, a grandparent can't. Don't you remember how much you resented your dad criticizing your performance in math/drama/sports, in the vain hope that by making clear his disappointment it would stimulate you to greater efforts? Whereas your

grandma took you aside, told you how wonderful you were, and confided that your dad was crap at math/ drama/sports, which is why he was so determined that you do better than he ever managed. My mother rarely praised us to our faces, maybe from a superstitious belief that if the gods heard her doing so they would punish her and us for pride, but she was generous in her support, and we knew she was proud of us when we found she had kept every report and review that mentioned our various activities. We in our turn lavishly praised and encouraged our daughters in almost everything they did—and I quickly discovered that withholding encouragement for some activity that in my opinion wasn't worthy of their efforts was ineffective and counterproductive. Now I praise our children and grandchildren unstintingly, and am careful to ensure that if criticism cannot in all conscience be avoided, it is constructive in nature.

Enemies are good for keeping the blood hot when you might otherwise chill into complacency. A proper enemy will last a lifetime, even when the original cause or quarrel has long been forgotten. Nobody enjoys becoming an enemy just for saying something they didn't mean, or doing something that was totally misinterpreted, but if your attempts at explanation are rejected, you've made an enemy whether you like it or not, and you have to choose between placating them (involving uncomfortable walks on eggshells), ignoring them, or showing them you're an enemy to be reckoned with. When you're young you swear revenge, but the great thing about growing older is that you can take your time. You know life will somehow punish your enemies even if you don't get around to it, and you always have in reserve the formidable weapon of forgiveness, which might crush them entirely.

Energy is like ground source heating: It doesn't run out but it needs to be properly channeled to be effective. Everyone admires the energy of those oldies who rush round tackling a million different things, even if they don't actually complete many of them. As someone with a low boredom threshold, as well as a butterfly mind, I don't think it's a waste of energy to take on a task I rapidly discover is beyond me. Indeed, I might say it was both a demonstration of my willingness to rise to a challenge and a sign of maturity to admit, if not defeat, then an admission, that the job needs someone who knows what they're doing.

It's not that at our age we've exhausted our supply of energy, except maybe where the use of our muscles is concerned; it's just that those of us who are still competitive and impatient should try to learn how to pace ourselves. As if.

Entrepreneurs: Is it ever too late to become an entrepreneur? I don't think so. Is it a good thing? That depends on whether your entrepreneurial attitude turns you from a reasonable human being into a bullying narcissist like Donald Trump or Alan Sugar, both of whom may be filthy rich but who are also intimately acquainted with bankruptcy. Experts (whom we all despise) say that a society run by entrepreneurs—people who take risks in order to make profits—will be more successful than one run either by multinational corporations or by the state. I've been my own boss—which isn't quite the same as being an entrepreneur, but close—since I was in my midtwenties, but even if you've been an employee all your working life, there's no reason why you can't become an entrepreneur when you retire. You can use your skills to be a consultant and offer advice based on long experience, or you can change direction entirely (which I did in my sixties) and build a business that

fills what you perceive to be a gap in the market. To do so you need confidence, contacts, and chutzpah, but I wouldn't risk raising any more capital than I could afford to lose. Once you're in the hands of the money men they'll have your integrity as well as your assets, and while risk can be exciting and stimulating, if you lose your humanity you lose everything that matters.

Envy is a bit ridiculous when we've gotten this far and achieved so much, but it still creeps in like mold on a damp wall. I think it starts with puberty—before that you just want what other children already have, which is desire (or greed) rather than resentment that you can't instantly enjoy what you covet. Once the hormones kick in, you realize that some people have qualities (wealth, straight hair, long legs, confidence with the opposite sex) that you lack and they don't really deserve, and that's when envy takes a hold. And even though we have done many things we can look back on with pride, there's always some niggling item, some trivial publicity given to a trifling achievement by someone who doesn't have a tenth of our talent, that undermines our sense of satisfaction. I cope with envy by telling myself I wouldn't want to be in their shoes, having to deal with all that (possibly hostile) attention after they exhaust themselves by relentlessly seeking the limelight; that I may not be as rich as some, but I can behave as I please and enjoy the loving support of my family and friends. If that isn't enviable, I don't know what is.

Excess is another of those things we should have learned how to manage, but somehow haven't gotten around to doing so. We know what harm it does; we've seen how it destroys other people's looks, health, and relationships; we've frequently experienced the disappointments and indigestion that invariably succeed overindulgence; and yet when we're on a roll we don't seem able to stop ourselves. We fool ourselves into believing that because we've gotten away with it before, we'll do so again, that we've earned the right to go over the top, that success and excess sound so similar the one rightly leads to the other. And we dismiss and decry the efforts of anyone who tries to stop us. When it comes to willpower (p. 207), those of us prone to excess are quite frankly pathetic, which makes it all the more amazing that we've gotten this far relatively unscathed.

Excuses are burnished by experience, but their shine grows dull with repetition. We can always invent a reason for being late for a stranger; try the same excuse on friends or family and you will be met with derision or worse. Most damaging of all is when, unable to convincingly excuse ourselves for doing something foolish or hurtful, we turn the blame on those we have let down. How could they not recognize the strain we've been under? How dare they attack us when we are so fragile? How can they not understand that we aren't always superhuman? When we know we've run out of excuses and refuse to acknowledge it, a relationship is threatened that could be salvaged with a simple apology (p. 11). If only everything were that easy.

Exercise should be pleasurable at our age. Its benefits are widely trumpeted, but all that crap about no gain without pain should be left to the young, as no amount of exercise is going to restore the youthful shape that we used to enjoy without fuss. I do three or four minutes' exercise every morning if possible— rolling my head around my hunched shoulders ten times to the left and right (crunching the cartilage is good for ironing out kinks), standing on my right foot for a count of twenty-five, then trying to do it with my eyes closed for a count of ten (surprisingly difficult but good for the brain), repeating that standing on my left foot, then doing at least thirty push-ups. I also try to walk a couple of miles every day, whatever the weather, and I do my best not to slouch and to keep the back of my head in line with my bum. It sometimes makes me puff a bit, especially going uphill, and if I don't feel any the worse for that, I don't always feel much better either. Getting through my daily routine is a little success, which—being an optimist—I hope will lead to further successes as the day unfolds. Even if it doesn't, it's a good start.

Expectations, like ambition (p. 9), don't seem to diminish with age, and nor should they. As long as you have something to look forward to, you will always be popular at parties where everyone else is depressed about the prospects of civilization in general and their own future in particular. A positive attitude is supposed to make you live longer, though it also requires good health, good friends, and, if possible, a good bank balance—the compost that keeps expectations warm.

Experts *See Amateurs.*

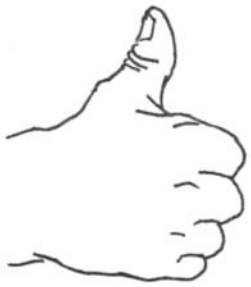

F

Farting has surely made people giggle ever since
our ancestors shared their caves with their animals,
and a child realized that their father and their ox
were indistinguishable when breaking wind. If you've
followed an elderly relative upstairs and giggled as they
farted unselfconsciously and without acknowledgment
or apology, take heed, because that will be you one day.
It's natural, if noxious—as a vegetarian, I can attest
that meat-free farts smell as bad as those prompted by
digested flesh—and they get worse as we grow older,
which is surely the origin of the derogatory term "old
fart." Controlling them is like restraining your belching

or your temper: Some people regard it as a sign of civilized behavior, but it really comes down to eating more slowly and, in the case of temper, thinking before you speak. If you haven't achieved such mastery at your time of life, you're hardly going to start now, are you?

Fashion continues to intrigue and annoy us even when we have outgrown the need to impress. Mature people who say they don't care about fashion are either liars or celebrity trendsetters; the rest of us fight a low-key, grumbling campaign to look up-to-date while retaining our individuality. When we had a job or an office to go to, we rarely wore the same things twice; now that it's no longer the case, we wear what is comfortable until dirt or boredom dictates a change. It's when we go out that the problems begin: What do we have that still fits, isn't laughably old-fashioned, and won't make us look as if we're trying too hard? Assuming it's not one of those occasions for which a whole new outfit is required, we are forced to go through a wardrobe full of things we haven't worn for years and can hardly wriggle into, yet we can't bear to throw away because we might one day lose enough weight to make them wearable, because they conjure up cherished memories, or because they cost a fair bit at the time and we all hate waste. Also, as we grow older, when we find something that suits us we often buy several versions of it just in case they discontinue the line, and that means even more stuff to wade through that is only good for slopping about in. We know we should do a proper clean-out, but that's another tedious chore (p. 38) to be postponed for as long as possible. It's sometimes enough to make even those who were once effortlessly fashionable dread going out. *See also Appearance.*

Fear seems to increase as we grow older, and can be quite paralyzing if you have no one to share it with. You would think that our long experience teaches us how to cope with most things, but of course we also know how much can go wrong and grow fearful—not just for ourselves and our failing powers, but even more for our children and grandchildren, who run risks we can hardly bear to contemplate. We all have acquaintances who've stopped accepting dinner invitations because they are fearful of driving at night; if they can't afford taxis and are wary of public transport, they can turn reclusive. We become careless with age, and it only takes a little accident, such as a fall, to make us afraid to take any risks at all. Like everything else, damage takes longer to heal when you're old, and that includes a return of confidence. Being honest and open about your fears may help, and your friends will laugh or encourage you to banish your worries. But if your fear has already isolated you, you will need the advice of a specialist, as you would with any condition that limited your activities.

Food is a pleasure that punishes you around the middle unless you are lucky enough to enjoy an active metabolism. Our grandparents wouldn't have understood the meaning of "obesity epidemic," because they knew, and may have experienced, genuine deprivation, and because the range of foods available to ordinary people was severely limited. They trusted fat men like Churchill or Alfred Hitchcock (though not film villains like Sydney Greenstreet) because they enjoyed their food and flaunted their success with their stomachs. Our parents, who had endured food rationing (and were the healthiest generation ever as a result), were more concerned about their figures, perhaps because they'd gotten used to making the best of what little was available (clothes were rationed, too). Many of our generation remember rationing in the UK in our formative years—I recall promising to end sweets rationing when standing as the Labour candidate in a school mock election: I got two votes, which briefly tempted me to declare myself a Conservative—but by the time we reached adulthood, food that had once been exotic and unobtainable was on offer in the new supermarkets that  were edging the old grocers out of existence. Yet we didn't become obese—that's the curse on the children brought up on sugary and fast food that we try to avoid. Of course, there's a new generation who are fanatical about eating healthily, and I'm sure they would dismiss my concern that taking food too seriously can stop you from enjoying it.

Forgetfulness is not necessarily a sign

of dementia (p. 51), but more often a failure of concentration. If you're the kind of person who likes routines (p. 169) to give shape and purpose to your day, you may start thinking of the task ahead instead of the one in hand, and the resultant "brain-slip" may cause you to forget what you were doing, especially if you're trying to talk at the same time. Couples who have been together for a long time often forget to finish their sentences, which can be maddening, though it also means they probably know what the other is going to say. Ellipsis, however, can also slide into forgetfulness, as the brain tries to cope with action as well as articulation, and it requires concentration to remember the point you'd started to develop. Forgetting facts, names, or faces, likewise, does not mean you're going senile or have a brain tumor. Your memory, like that of a computer, is incapable of giving instant access to the huge mass of information you have accumulated and stored over the years: It needs prompts, which in my case means going through the alphabet, sometimes several times, until a letter prompts the memory of a name, or something like it, which will, given time, drop into focus. In a way, forgetfulness is a tribute to the breadth of knowledge we have acquired with age. As with our other valued possessions, we store the stuff we don't have room to display, and it can take a little while to remember where we put it.

Fucking was the rudest word imaginable when we were young; now it is the commonest. Novelists who used the word used to be prosecuted for obscenity, whereas now it is so much a part of everyday speech that when you hear someone say, "Fuck the fucking fucker 'cos it's fucking fucked," you know what they mean. Our grandchildren say it and when they are rebuked they claim to have learned it from their parents. I cringe when people of my generation use it to appear cool; I know I drop it into conversation far too often; and when used in its original meaning, I think it's far too crude a word to do justice to the delicate sexual maneuvers we occasionally perform. Fuck it, I'm sounding like a prude.

G

Games are not things I excel at, either as a participant or a spectator. My grandmother played solitaire, my mother enjoyed bridge when my father died, my neighbor took up lawn bowling in her sixties because her new husband was a keen player, and another neighbor developed a fondness for watching pool in her nineties. I was hopeless at ball games, but I try to appear interested in rugby because my son-in-law, and hence my grandson, are both devotees. Mind you, the rules have changed so much since my schooldays I have to ask my daughter what's going on. I understand the benefits of joining in a competitive game that tests the mind rather than the muscles, and I admire people who can spend entire evenings playing bridge, which has always seemed to me like yachting—a mysterious pleasure whose rules are hard to acquire and whose players shout at you when you make a mistake. I like the idea of spending hours watching a sport and being passionately involved and informed, but I quickly get bored and feel I should be doing something else. We've surely reached the age when we shouldn't feel guilty about what does and doesn't give us pleasure, and as long as it doesn't harm others we are entitled to choose our own games, and play on our own if that's what gives us satisfaction.

Generosity is when you stop keeping score
and do something for the sheer pleasure of it rather than because it's your turn to splurge or perform a chore usually done by others. A generous gesture should be spontaneous and can be small—making an unexpected meal—or large, like surprising someone you love with something they really wanted. Love is supposed to flourish on mutual acts of competitive generosity, which is fine as long as neither side tries

to claim victory. And though the most delightful form of generosity may be giving to your children or grandchildren, you have to be scrupulously fair and make sure they all think they're getting things of equal value, or you will make enemies of those you only wanted to please.

Genes aren't always reliable. My mother was 103 and scarcely had a day's illness in her life; my father died at eighty-one, having swum twelve lengths of an Olympic-sized pool. So in theory, their three children should live to 102 (according to a formula in which you add the ages at which your parents died, divide them by 2 and add 10), yet my brother died at sixty-three of an autoimmune disease, and my late sister and I had four kinds of cancer between us. Of course there's no doubt we've all inherited certain features and characteristics of our parents—I see my father in the mirror when I shave, and I certainly have his geniality and impatience, as well as my mother's ability

to forget unpleasant occurrences—but to explain is not to excuse. We can and do blame our parents for most things, as our children blame us for passing on attitudes and behaviors that others censure, but nobody can yet determine how much is biological and how much is due to the environment in which we grew up. My view is that we should credit the genes for the good stuff we can do nothing about, and accept responsibility for the less good in the optimistic hope of changing it. I know it sounds like the AA program, but hey, if it works, don't knock it, right?

Grandchildren, apart from being adorable and adoring, at least when they're young and haven't been let down (not by us, of course), are completely fascinating because we can study them with a certain amount of distance. Of course we took a huge interest in our own children's intellectual and physical growth, but there was so much else going on—not least our own careers—that being objective about their achievements and failures was almost impossible. But you can watch your grandchildren develop their own personalities and see them react to their siblings and friends in such an individual fashion that you are frequently caught between marveling how alike they are to the parent you gave birth to and wondering where on earth they got that appalling temper (obviously from your child's partner). Because we forget so much of the important details of our own children's upbringing, it often seems as if our grandchildren are slower than they were at learning how to read and write, though their ability to handle anything with a touchscreen is extraordinary. But of course we keep our suspicions to ourselves, as even the slightest whisper of criticism or questioning their rate of development will lead to estrangement and maybe even denial of access, which would be an unimaginable deprivation. See also Encouragement.

Gratitude is something we have surely learned

not to expect. As my father used to say, we should be grateful not to be kicked in the teeth. Being grateful isn't the same as being polite—kids aren't made to write thank you letters the way we were, which may be bad manners, but those letters were only for form's sake, to ensure the supply of presents didn't dry up, and were hardly on a par with the gratitude we feel when we're helped out of an unexpected jam, or are the recipient of a surprising act of kindness (p. 113).

Different again is the gratitude we feel when we're told we don't have a fatal disease, or we get an unexpected bonus. We soon realize that the person or company who gave us the good news was just doing their job, whereas true gratitude is surely the pleasure we get from a generous and helpful action that is individual, impromptu, and offered without thought of gain. Of course we are grateful for our health, the love of friends and family, and even the qualities (and possibly the legacy) that our parents bestowed on us, but unless you're religious, to whom do you express your gratitude? You could simply offer heartfelt thanks for a generous gesture, and hope that if you were called on to perform something similar, you, too, would receive the gratitude you deserve.

Gravity, sadly, is all-conquering at our age and can only be defied with artificial aids or rigorous self-discipline. Eventually everything droops, even earlobes, which in some people grow pendulous. And while a woman can choose from a variety of bras, no one has yet invented a support for man boobs. Some older men have a problem with their testicles swelling and swinging, which gives a misleading impression of their potency. It's usually harmless fluid (but worth checking out) that can be drained, though it will probably return. As for the aging penis, droopy seems to be its natural state, and though there are pills that can make it perk up, which should be good for all concerned, introducing medical intervention an hour in advance of foreplay requires a degree of planning (and optimism) that can be off-putting for both parties, as well as inducing mild hysteria at the absurdity of it all. But it's the belly where all our indulgences decide to hang out: You can have liposuction, but if you've managed to avoid Botox, why bother with more expensive treatment whose effects are hardly long lasting? Of course we can and do fight nature, but assuming we're not talking about clinical obesity, isn't it more tempting to acknowledge that gravity has us comfortably beat?

Greed is a compulsion that affects all but the most saintly of us. Its appetite for more only grows with feeding. It's by no means limited to food and drink: Who has not, having once tasted praise, love, riches, or power, wanted more of them? It may be an evolutionary instinct, an urge to cram more in of whatever's available in case of dearth, but that's an explanation, not an excuse. Greed and laziness (p. 115) are two things you can't legislate against, and you can be certain that when people shamelessly exploit legal loopholes for personal gain, most of us are too lazy to protest because part of us wishes we'd done it, too. You would think that in our maturity we would know when we'd had enough, and stop wanting more than we could possibly need or use, but sadly that isn't often the case. We decry the greed of company bosses who regularly receive raises and bonuses that are not only hundreds of times more than their workers' wages but are grotesquely unrelated to performance, yet we are still greedy for a better deal on a new TV or a little boost to our pension, while grumbling if we have to pay more taxes. We could, and morally should, fight this compulsion and say we don't want more, but we tell ourselves we're only looking for what we deserve, and would never seek to deprive others of their just share. This is merely the difference between the gourmet and the glutton: The former claims to have a sophisticated palate while the latter is just a greedy bastard.

Grief *See Bereavement.*

Guilt is a chronic condition you can either blithely deny you suffer from or succumb to entirely. Of course we have all done things we should feel guilty about, and aside from those religious people who go to confession and atone with a few Hail Marys, most of us tend to cover our sins in layers of excuses until their sharp little edges are muffled. We may (or may not) make reparations but we quickly regard ourselves as rehabilitated, until a further sin—often affecting those we love (for we are not always perfect)—brings on another attack of guilt that requires a flurry of apologies before both the offended party and the guilty one return to equilibrium. But this cycle is easier to live with than those who insist everything is their fault. If there's an argument, they take the blame; if an accident occurs, they insist they caused it, whether there's a riot or a

refugee problem they feel guilty about it. There are few things more annoying than somebody who feeds on blame. It's pure attention seeking, and they are right to feel guilty.

Gullibility shouldn't affect people like us, who got where we are today by knowing our asses from our elbows. Yet we're always reading about people of our age who are conned by shoddy builders or bogus financial advisers or, most frequently, internet scammers. We tell ourselves we wouldn't be gulled, but if we were alone, or lonely, and someone came to the door, flashed some form of identity we're too polite to check properly, and offered to sort out our leaky guttering for a few dollars in cash, would we resist? Would we say no to someone who insisted he wasn't trying to sell us anything, he just wanted us to be aware of an unparalleled investment opportunity that someone with our experience would recognize as safe and sensible? And while of course we delete those emails that tell us we've won some lottery or are owed some tax refund, if we would just give them our bank details, who can ignore the offers of insurance that are so much lower than anything we've been quoted? It's hard enough to put down the phone on a cold

caller, especially if they're raising money for a charity, but we're all gullible in the face of a bit of flattery and an appeal to our better nature.

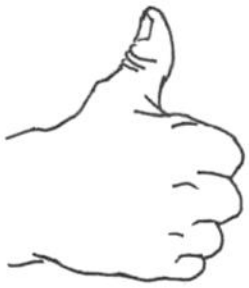

Hallucinations are not confined to the drunk or drugged. When my mother was over 100 and spent most of her time in bed, she often saw people looking down on her from the ceiling, whom we couldn't see, as well as being convinced she had visits from several men claiming to be her husband, who'd been dead for a quarter of a century. She didn't find these hallucinations alarming or upsetting but merely puzzling, and we decided they were the product of boredom and a rich imagination. I'm sure many of us find ourselves, when alone, talking to friends or relatives who have died, and it's rather comforting if, through a trick of the light or the shifting of shadows, we see shapes that resemble them, even though we know they're not really there. They're not threatening, unlike figures in nightmares, and they're not a sign of madness—they may even be a welcome escape from the tedium of daytime TV repeats.

Handwriting is hardly used by those who

prefer computers, but I still scribble notes in my own version of shorthand. Both my parents had beautiful, and very different, handwriting, which remained perfectly legible almost until they died; I learned a sort of bastard italic, which looked distinguished but is very hard for others to read. Our daughters have developed their own styles, which are immediately recognizable and more legible than mine. Most people of our own generation handwrite Christmas cards, whereas those a little younger send printed ones, which seems rather impersonal. Our handwriting is a sign of our character and individuality, even if it has grown a little shaky; we can still be expressive applying ink to paper, though of course even two-fingered typists find a keyboard can keep up with their thoughts better than a pen. Few of us write letters anymore, except for those of condolence, and thanks to the tremors of age I have taken to typing those—with reluctance (a handwritten note shows how much you care), but also with relief that the recipient will not have to strain to discern my meaning. It's fascinating to look at old manuscripts and see how the writer changed their mind through their deletions and insertions, and though it's infinitely easier to edit on a computer, all your changes vanish into a limbo only a nerd can access. At present children are taught how to write by hand, but how long will that last when even computer-generated signatures are now acceptable? Then what will happen when there's a power failure and you still need to communicate? Or when changes to technology make it impossible for tomorrow's machines to read today's program? Handwriting will be around for as long as books, so if you've still got your fountain pen, keep it filled.

Health *See Ailments.*

History can be an excuse for inaction, even complacency. We allow ourselves to think that because we have survived, and are more civilized and educated than history's victims, we would never share their fate. We have lived long enough to know that what goes around comes around, and even if we were activists in our youth, we settle back in our chairs, telling ourselves that we've done our bit and now it's the turn of the younger generation. But we know that history repeats itself, and that our survival depends more on chance and luck than on education and culture, and that should get us up and running again. With all our experience, we need to keep making history, not content ourselves with merely being part of it.

Hobbies are supposed to be what we fill our leisure hours with, especially in retirement, but who has time? Our parents knew they would give up full-time work in their sixties and devote themselves to travel or bridge or gardening or taking an adult education course, but our generation already labors for more years than our parents did to qualify for our pensions. Now recession and austerity have diminished

our savings, and they've also affected the provision of classes where you burnish your skills or acquire new ones. That lovely picture of a white-haired couple walking footpaths hand in hand, or of an old geezer in a cardigan and slippers making a model of the Eiffel Tower from matchsticks while his wife does tai chi, has been replaced by the more frenetic activities of those of us who are busy trying to survive financially as well as emotionally. Hobbies are now just a part of our lives, not the whole point of it.

Homosexuality: A friend of ours waited until

he was fifty to come out, grow his receding hair until it was long enough for a ponytail, buy a convertible sports car, and leave his wife and children for a guy who lived by the sea. He was of the generation above us; now we are neither surprised nor shocked when a friend who is a grandparent moves in with someone of the same sex, and may even marry them. Increasing numbers of young people say they're unsure of their sexuality, which isn't something we would have admitted when we were their age, though most of us at some point admired people of our own sex, even if we never did anything about it. Yet cultural attitudes have changed so much that we see gay people of our generation being proud, outspoken, and in the forefront of protests against prejudice, which shows that our fight for civilized values still counts for something.

Honesty can turn around and bite you. An actor we knew had an affair on tour and, being convinced his wife would find out about it anyway, revealed the fact to her. He was astonished when she threw him out and later divorced him. I rather admired his honesty, and said as much to my own wife, who surprised me by retorting she thought our friend was pathetic, acting like a little boy and confessing. I said surely people should be honest with one another; she said not if they were going to betray their partner and then think they could just own up and get away with it. So, "If I had an affair you'd rather not know?" I asked. "I'd rather you didn't have an affair in the first place," she replied.

Hormones can be blamed for everything, though at our age their roar has been reduced to a muffled cough. Most women of our generation are no longer treated with hormone replacement therapy (HRT) and the only hormone men are treated to is estrogen to fight off prostate cancer. Yet we are still perfectly capable of emotional and irrational behavior, despite our hormones being comatose. The rage of an elderly person can be fierce and frightening, and if it's not a chemical thing it can be provoked by resentment at being taken for granted. Which is a salutary surprise to the young, who are still in thrall to their hormonal urges. *See also Moods.*

Humor is such a personal thing, one reader's giggle being another's groan, that I will limit myself to saying that if you can't see the funny side of growing older, despite its limitations, afflictions, and absurdities, I hope you were given this book as a gift rather than splurging on it yourself.

Hygiene is crucial if you don't want to smell old as well as suffering from the infections that take root if you don't wash your cracks and crevices. We get used to our own odors, just as we take for granted our little idiosyncrasies and infirmities, whereas someone we haven't seen for a while, but who knows us well, will wrinkle their nose (or, if they know us well enough, actually complain) at the stink. It's a bit like being a small child again, but you have to pay attention to behind the ears, under the arms, and between the legs and toes. You're old enough to know when you need fresh clothes, sheets, and towels, and though it may be tempting to listen to those who say frequent washing is damaging to our immune system, you're surely going to keep washing your hair regularly until arthritis or some other ailment means you have to ask someone to do it for you.

Hypochondria is what other people have, wasting the doctor's time with imaginary problems. Whereas we know when we're ill. Our problem is finding a doctor who won't just listen, nodding sympathetically, and then say, "It's your age, I'm afraid," but who will find the root cause of what is obviously a serious malady and immediately supply a cure. Or at least refer us to a specialist.

Hypocrisy isn't when you tell an actor they were wonderful when they were terrible, or a politician that they have a point when they're plainly raving, or a friend that they look terrific when they're deathly ill. That's being well-mannered for the sake of a quiet life, and because we all want to be liked. Hypocrisy is when you promise you'll go and see someone you have no desire or intention to visit; when you say you'd love to have lunch with someone you've successfully avoided for months; when you add to an email "Do let me know if there's anything more I can do" when you've plainly washed your hands of the matter. Hypocrisy is lying, and nonetheless reprehensible when you do it at a distance. We're all guilty, and the worst part is we've gotten so used to it we're no longer bothered.

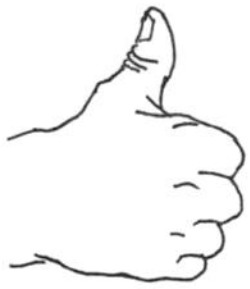

I

Ignorance at our time of life tends to be willful and deliberate rather than the result of a lack of education or interest. Having made a reasonable success of our lives so far, we choose to be ignorant of things that bore us (such as the latest technology—what are grandchildren for?), annoy us (such as the latest politics—seen it all before), or we can do little about (such as illness—all we want is for the doctor to tell us we'll be fine). We should still have the intellectual energy to find out about stuff we care about, but given the deluge of information available, ignorance can be a useful umbrella to hide under.

Impotence can of course be remedied with
little pills, but it's still hurtful to a man's pride and
confidence. We can explain it away as the result of
age or drink or cancer therapy, we can—in the right
company—laugh it off, but it's no fun having a major
disconnect between what the mind wants and what
the body delivers. If you love someone, you want to
pay them the compliment of showing how desirable
and arousing they are, and though I know there are
techniques that allow for a satisfactory coupling—and
non-penetrative sex can be perfectly satisfactory—we
still mourn the lost simplicity of a decent erection.

Incontinence *See Dribbling.*

Infidelity *See Betrayal.*

In-laws remain a problem even when our
children are serenely settled. I've tried to avoid gender
stereotyping, but I think it's fair to say that for most
fathers no man is quite good enough for his daughter,
just as for most mothers no woman is going to treat her
son the way he deserves. Most fathers can be bribed
into acceptance with the odd present from the son-
in-law, or persuaded by evidence of their daughter's

happiness that he's not as bad as first thought; mothers are harder to convince. But if you want to enjoy your grandchildren, you not only have to accept that your son- or daughter-in-law knows their children better than you do, you should also lavish praise on them for bringing your grandchildren up so brilliantly. Keep your criticism for your closest and most discreet friends, and never comment on your in-laws' parents—the outlaws?—unless, of course, their offspring invite you to do so. Even then it is wise to be cautious, as your remarks will undoubtedly be used as ammunition should a battle begin.

Insomnia comes in two forms: the one that has

you tossing and turning and desperate to get to sleep, and the one where you wake up feeling perfectly rested even though it's still dark outside. The first is probably best dealt with by a pill or other therapy to restore your normal sleep pattern; the trick with the other is not to worry about it. I used to sleep for eight hours but

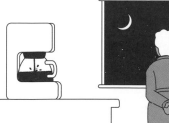

now find I'm absolutely fine with five or six. I could get up, but what would I do in the middle of the night that isn't better done in daylight? I could read, thanks to Kindle, without disturbing my wife, but whereas she gets frazzled if she can't get her eight hours, I'm happy lying in the warm and letting my mind skitter off in every direction. If I feel I could do with another couple of hours' sleep, I relax from the top of my head downward, lying on my back or my side, unclenching my jaw, unlocking my shoulders and loosening my chest, especially my lungs, so I don't snuffle or snore, settling my hips, stomach, knees, ankles, and toes into the mattress, and try a mantra I invented: mentally muttering "just" as I breathe in, and "sleep" as I breathe out. Concentrating on one monosyllable as I inhale and another as I exhale—I also envisage windshield wipers working intermittently to clear away extraneous thoughts—seems to act as a simple tether on the mind, and I know it's worked only when I wake up realizing I've had a dream or two. Otherwise I welcome whatever thoughts choose to settle, without worrying about following up on them.

The mind processes things even when you're not concentrating on them, and will remember or recall the ideas that matter. I get up when it's light, and I don't feel tired because I trust my body to know when it's had enough rest. Of course, it doesn't always work. If it did, I would be so serene I'd be insufferable. But whereas when I was young I couldn't bear not to be doing or thinking about something productive, I've now reached an age when I feel my brain, having been required to focus on so much for so long, deserves the right to occasionally roam freely. I've also learned not to tell people who complain at being unable to sleep that all they need to do is relax.

Instinct can't be acquired—we have to learn to trust it. That we've survived this far is a sign we've managed to do so, and also of how we've successfully played instinct off against intellect. Of course, some instincts let us down and manifest themselves in inappropriate behavior or, worse, simple failure (see Impotence), but our instinct and experience also teach us to distrust experts, as when we're prescribed pills that make us feel worse, or spun policies that appeal to the crude instinct to punish people weaker than we are. I believe that most people are instinctively inclined to treat others as they would be like to be treated, but then I'm also by instinct an optimist.

Intellect is acquired through education and example, but if it isn't tempered by instinct (p. 107), it's about as persuasive as a robot rapping. I was expensively educated, but my successes came about only when I trusted my instinct more than my intellect. As we grow older we have to guard against relying only on what our intellect and experience has taught us, because that may no longer be fit for purpose. To stay alert and mentally alive we have to knock the barnacles off our instincts and take the risk of doing at least some of the stuff our intellect tells us is dangerous. We may fail or look foolish, but we might also have fun.

J

Jogging is a form of exercise I abhor. I know of people in their seventies who play tennis competitively, and have seen centenarians running marathons, but those activities have point and purpose. Jogging, however, that mechanical pounding in absurdly expensive sneakers that jars your spine and strains your knees and tendons, that lacks the grace of running or vigorous walking—to me it's as ridiculous as speed walking for mature people. Though who am I to spoil anyone's enjoyment?

Jokes bear endless repetition, as long as you remember the punchline. Our partners and friends have probably heard us tell the same joke a thousand times: The former will raise a loyal eyebrow, the latter will groan but indulge you as long as you don't fuck it up. As for the young, or strangers willing to listen to you, just remember that if you're going to have to explain the historical or cultural references in order to make your political incorrectness funny, you'd be better off shutting up and buying a round of drinks.

Being **judgmental** is extraordinarily tempting, given how much we've learned over the years, and how ready we are to put people right, but it can also damage our reputation and credibility. We've been taught not to jump to conclusions before we're in full possession of the facts, but if, like me, you get more impatient as you grow older, you probably find yourself unable to wait until you've heard all the arguments to express your opinion. If you then come under attack, you defend yourself with a smokescreen of indignation that obscures the facts that should alter your perspective. But while legal judgments are subject to appeal, personal ones can end friendships. Take sides in a divorce, and condemn one of the parties, even lightheartedly, and those who once regarded your judgment as trustworthy will attack you as a prejudiced bigot whose opinion is worthless. Is that going to stop us from giving our views in a manner we believe is forthright and others attack as bombast? Sadly, maturity and wisdom are not always natural bedfellows.

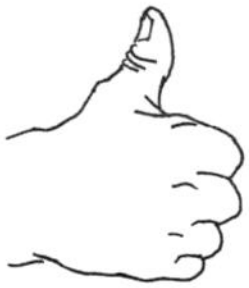

Kindness can be directed inward as well as outward. Being kind to yourself is not self-indulgence; it's validating your own worth. We are probably our own harshest critics, and certainly we know our own limitations better than anyone, so when an action we thought would be helpful is hurtfully misinterpreted as interference, it is a kindness to remind ourselves that our intentions were honorable. Not everything that goes wrong is our fault, and while we are good at taking the blame for the sake of a peaceful life, being kind to ourselves means sharing the burden of guilt that from time to time cripples us all.

L

Laughter is life enhancing as long as you don't choke. There are few tragedies that don't have their funny side, and the good taste we have acquired over the years allows us to point them out at an appropriate moment. Or possibly an inappropriate one: Another advantage of age is that you can frequently get away with being outrageous, though the charm wears off if you do it too often.

Laziness should not be confused with idleness or wasting time (p. 206), which are necessary indulgences to conserve our mental and physical strength. Laziness consists of not doing things that need to be done because you no longer care about the consequences, or rely on others doing them for you. It can happen when you're depressed or lonely and of course all right-thinking people should resist and fight it. Just try telling them so.

Listening is one of the most important things we can do in our maturity. It's the most effective form of therapy, as well as the cheapest, as everyone likes talking about themselves to someone who is experienced and nonjudgmental. Advice (p. 5) may be sought, though just putting words to fears and follies and being heard is healing in itself. But as with gratitude (p. 85), don't expect to be listened to in return. If you are, that's a bonus, but most people are so relieved to have unburdened themselves, they don't want to know any more.

Lists are an essential part of our lives: They give us purpose, structure and satisfaction. Therapists say making a daily list of what you want to achieve, and ticking items off, boosts self-esteem and confidence, though your ambitions have to be commensurate with your abilities—set the bar too high and you'll end up feeling even more of a failure. Lists are also vital for those whose memory needs jogging. On the one hand, writing something down removes the need to carry it in your overstuffed head (provided, of course, you remember where you've put the list); on the other, memory is like a muscle that grows flabby if not exercised. I used to be an inveterate list maker, writing ideas down on scraps of paper, which I would attempt to file by subject, though most were so random, and so readily superseded by subsequent thoughts, that I stopped bothering. I now take the view that stuff will be remembered if it's important enough (though at night I sometimes cheat by making a note in the air, which seems to make it last until the morning), and save my lists for work and shopping.

Loneliness

is a condition that's hard to understand if you're not a sufferer. Solitariness—people who prefer and are perfectly happy with their own company—we can comprehend, but the lonely are a problem few of us want to tackle. We make sure friends who've been bereaved are looked after, calling round with meals they wouldn't bother to cook for themselves, but after a while we stop phoning and leave them to their own devices. We can cope with their grief, but we soon want to shake off the chill of their isolation, in case it's catching. Yet the truly lonely—those who try to manage on their own but because of illness or poverty are unable to leave their homes—are growing in number. Of course, if we all made regular visits to someone we knew had no one else, the world would be a kinder place. But how many of us have the time and dedication required? *See also Solitude.*

Losing is something you have to do with grace, but if you haven't learned that by now you never will. Losing to a lover, or small children, may be a deliberate act of generosity (p. 82), but if you can't bear losing to a friend, then enjoy your tantrum, or learn to cheat better.

Love, if you're lucky, deepens with age. It means you can still be surprised after years of familiarity by an aspect of beauty (p. 20), by failings that have become endearing, by a sudden vulnerability you yearn to protect, by generosity, tolerance, and understanding beyond what you deserve, which you hope you return with interest. It also means sharing physical and emotional intimacy without shame or inhibition, and having someone to tell anything to, however trivial or absurd. The loss of such a love tears you in half. You can recover, and new love is always possible. Just don't expect it to be the same.

Luck has to be recognized, then grabbed before it can get away. Experience makes this easier, though not always. Luck isn't the same as chance (p. 34), which is random. If someone calls you lucky, it's a compliment, whereas describing you as a chancer means you're not to be trusted, even if you are successful. When people envy your luck, they ignore the defeats you've suffered and the sadness you've endured, not realizing that luck is a bit like cooking: You can add a new ingredient to a familiar recipe and it's either a triumph or a dish best forgotten.

Lust lurks around even the most aged of us, though desire rarely leads to performance. It can be explained as an instinct beyond our rational control, to be endured like any other ache you can do little about. *See also Arousal.*

Lying is a sin we all commit because experience has taught us that honesty (p. 98) can be destructive. We don't tell a loved one who's unsure about a new hairstyle that it makes them look old and stupid, or a child who presents you with a drawing that a baboon armed with a crayon could have done better. Truth can be overrated, especially when most of us hear only what we want to hear. On the other hand, we owe it to our principles to expose lying when politicians start trading in "fake facts." Most of us have survived this far by not sticking our heads too far above the parapet, but we have to become fighters for truth when lying becomes part of the political culture, because how else will those who come after us know the false from the true?

M

Manners are a bit like language: You learn from those around you, and though your interpretation might change, you stick by the rules you acquired in childhood, unless forced to behave differently. Why do they matter? Because manners are a code by which like recognizes like and can engage with them despite deep differences of opinion; because good manners—which involve politeness, respect, and a degree of good-humored tolerance (p. 192)—allow you to get away with doing and saying outrageous things, which is an enormous pleasure at our age; and because bad manners are a blight on our culture, and we ought to at least try to set an example of how to behave better.

Marriage seems to work for around half the population, and though our generation maintained it didn't matter whether or not you signed a piece of paper provided the relationship was sound, my wife and I were surprised when both our daughters opted for formal vows, citing the comfort of commitment. Equally surprising is the number of people of our age who marry again, after the divorce or death of their partner, or when coming out as gay. You would think they would be happy just living together, as a marriage certificate isn't going to affect their relationship as much as, say, a prenuptial agreement. But standing up in public and swearing to love, cherish, and stick with your partner until death do you part is a lovely thing to do, provided you believe in what you're saying and work at making it happen. It also makes it easier for your heirs to sort out their inheritance, but of course that wasn't on your mind. . . .

Masturbation doesn't make you blind, but it's certainly habit-forming. In our youth, we were told—especially if you were a Boy Scout, and maybe Girl Scouts were taught the same—that it was an evil act that sapped the strength and led to eternal damnation, which perhaps explained its attraction, along of course with the exquisite pleasure it gave. Babies play with themselves naturally, and if you hadn't learned by puberty what to do with your bits and pieces, friends would surely teach you. Actual intercourse never stopped masturbation between bouts, as it has always been a rapid form of relief that was free of fuss or worry about giving pleasure to anyone other than yourself. Now that intercourse is a rarer occurrence, masturbation is still available, and though like most things it takes longer and doesn't always offer the satisfaction it once did, we are surely old enough not to feel guilty about it.

Meditation is, so I'm told, effective in relieving stress. But if you're not in the habit of doing it, and doing it properly, will you have the patience at your time of life to sit down and learn a new way of thinking that may not deliver on its promises? I'm not being cynical—on the contrary, I respect and mildly envy people who can find inner peace—but it seems to me to be one of those things that if you haven't given it a go by now in your search for enlightenment, you've left it a bit late. *See also Mindfulness.*

Memory is like a vast swamp, impressive, and treacherous. You can stride across it sure-footed, and remember everything when you want to, but at other times your feet are sucked into the ooze and you can barely recall a thing. Comfort yourself that forgetting things is not necessarily a sign of senility or a brain tumor, and nor is remembering things from your past when you can barely call to mind what you did yesterday. It may just be that yesterday was quite boring. *See also Forgetfulness.*

Metabolism slows down in most people as you grow older, and there's nothing you can do about it. We all envy the few who boast they can eat and drink as much as they like and still stay slim, though we'd secretly like to think they're probably alcoholics or drug addicts and miserably unhappy even though their dress size or waist hasn't changed since they were pimply teenagers. Metabolism is a spiteful process that punishes normal people like you and me even though we drink half of what we used to and claim to rigidly control our eating. If they came up with a pill to revitalize our metabolism it would probably give us cancer, so we just have to suck it up. Intelligent design, ha! It's enough to drive anyone to drink.

Mindfulness, as I understand it, is the opposite of meditation (p. 123), in that it gets you to concentrate on yourself, your actions, and the reasons behind them, instead of putting self aside in favor of higher matters. Great claims are made for mindfulness, especially when used in conjunction with cognitive behavioral therapy, and I can see why taking the time and trouble to analyze your behavior; to be aware of what has stressed, depressed, or made you angry; and to understand and appreciate the effect your moods are having on others can only make for better communication and more positive interaction between civilized people. Of course it's not going to stop you from having a turn or losing control when things, as they so frequently do, get on top of you, but it's something to bear in mind when the storm has passed. We're not all sensible enough to carry an umbrella in case it rains, and in a storm good intentions won't stop you from getting wet, but if you accept that by not taking precautions you have only yourself to blame for your shoes getting soaked, that's a welcome indication of self-awareness.

Mistakes are signs of vitality, inventiveness, and an adventurous intelligence, at least when we ourselves make them. You'll never try or discover something new if you're afraid of getting it wrong. Mistakes are an unavoidable part of progress, whether or not we learn from them. Unfortunately, we have developed a litigious culture that leads to any professional having their ass sued if what they did, or advised, was in any way damaging. Obviously incompetence or malpractice deserves punishment, but the young should be aware that when we make mistakes, it's a sign that we prefer experiment to being cautious to the point of cowardice (p. 43).

Moderation is incredibly boring if you stick to it all the time. It may be sensible and necessary and good for our bodies as well as the environment, but where's the fun in being human if you can't occasionally go wild at our age? Especially when we're confident we can compensate for our excesses by depriving ourselves until things are back in balance. Have that extra chocolate—you're only finishing a box you would never have bought for yourself, and it might be weeks before someone buys you some more.

M

Modesty can be unbecoming in people of our accomplishments. We shouldn't boast, but nor should we play down the significance of what we've achieved. The trick is to do it through hints that lead to your audience wanting more, in a display of what I might call provocative modesty, as in a striptease. Show them everything and they immediately lose interest; drop tempting titbits of information that subtly reveal how successful you are, and they'll eat out of your hand. This doesn't work if you have little to be modest about, but surely you can bullshit better than they can?

Moisturizer is not something I thought I would ever recommend, but since it's now as fashionable for men as for women, I tried it, and it's really quite pleasant. I can't say that I owe my youthful complexion to it, because that's down to genes, a daily walk in all weather, and an ability to avoid worrying (or frowning) about things I can't alter. But rubbing creamy stuff onto my skin after a shave has become part of my routine, and provided it doesn't become outrageously expensive I shall carry on. And to think when I was young I used to take a bath once a week in which I washed my body and hair with a simple bar of soap . . .

Money allows you to enjoy life if you have enough, and a bit over. But you don't become filthy rich without doing some dastardly things, and once a dastard, always a dastard. Though even the most reasonable of us can't entirely escape greed (p. 88) in our maturity, hopefully we've given up chasing every last penny in favor of spreading our cash among those we love. And keeping some aside in case things turn sour.

Moods may no longer be caused by hormones (p. 98) as we age, but brain chemistry that no one quite understands can cause emotional swerves that are just as violent and desperate as when we were teenagers. A tiny incident can provoke a major explosion in someone who is usually as affable as they are unflappable; equally common is a fit of depression in people who may never have suffered from it before. The cause may be bereavement, the breakup of a relationship, the death of a pet, a chronic ailment the doctors can neither explain nor cure, or the realization that at our age we have to face the prospect of failure as well as mortality. Or a normally sunny mood can suddenly turn chill for no reason whatsoever. The important thing is to accept that if chemicals can cause the mood to change for the worse, there are also chemicals and

herbal remedies that can improve it, or at least blunt
its edge. Most of us don't like taking pills, but while we
submit to medicine for a physical problem, swallowing
tablets for a mental problem feels like an admission of
weakness—which is ridiculous if they work, if they're
not fraudulent or clash with other stuff you're taking,
and if you believe they will actually help.

Morality only works by example, and any attempt
to impose it on others is bound to fail, especially if
your would-be victim has access to your history. *See
also Advice.*

N

Nakedness is fine if you're a naturist or in a tolerant and understanding relationship, but is otherwise not recommended unless you are extremely fit or blind to your own imperfections.

Napping is an art you may acquire with age. My father used to fall asleep after a meal, occasionally at the table, and regularly at the movies or theater, though he would join enthusiastically in the applause. I never took naps after being forced to do so as a child, and if I occasionally fell asleep after a heavy lunch I would always wake with a crick in my neck and a sour taste in my mouth. That is, until my seventies, when a short nap during the television news extended—without any deliberate action on my part—to the occasional ten-minute snooze at my desk or on the train. I allow my head to fall forward, which is more comfortable than those ergonomic headrests on trains designed for, and probably by, robots, and miraculously wake up feeling refreshed. This happy acquisition of a practice that is healthy, natural, requires no professional expertise, and is free coincided with a shortening of the hours of sleep I seemed to need. Which at least demonstrates that there are some advantages to aging. *See also Insomnia.*

Nostalgia is being in love with the past, and old loves almost always disappoint. You go through old photographs, you marvel at how lithe and lovely you were, you perhaps remember with a pang at how involved you were in politics and protests, but then you think how the progress you fought for has been rolled back, and mutter your disappointment at the failure of the young to march for the things you cared about. You ramble on about how your childhood was full of long hot summers, whereas in reality you sat on windy beaches in an itchy woolen swimsuit, whipped by sand

and salt, sickened by the smell of gas and fry grease, surrounded by people you'd run a mile to avoid, and bored out of your mind. You sigh for the days when you looked things up in a book with pages you could turn and ink you could smell, whereas now you can find anything in seconds on the internet, and some of it is even reliable. In the old days we were taut with energy, stamina, and ambition, and we used them to grow into what we've become. Now we can be comfortable with things that are looser and more suited to a relaxed but vigilant attitude. That's surely something to be proud of rather than to regret.

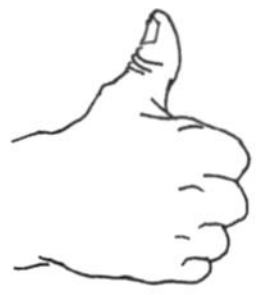

Obsessions can govern your life, as opposed to routines (p. 169), which merely help it to run smoothly. If you become obsessed by the order in which you shower, brush your teeth, and perform the other necessities of your rising ritual, when the order is interrupted or interfered with you can be unsettled for the rest of the day, or even rendered incapable of functioning normally. Obsessions are emotional crutches that come to govern your moods and behavior rather than helping you to remain in control: You can only loosen their stifling grip by becoming sufficiently self-aware to understand how they arose and how you can diminish their influence. *See also Mindfulness.*

Optimism can be acquired with effort, though it's basically a product of inheritance and encouragement. In publishing, optimism is endemic among editors (though tempered by the caution some would call cowardice of the men in suits), and with writers, optimism usually strays into fantasy about becoming bestsellers. When I changed careers in my sixties and became a literary agent, encouraged by my wife who is a realist with a streak of pessimism, it never occurred to me that I wouldn't succeed. My optimism was bolstered by experience (as well as contacts), but I was also dealing with other people's work rather than my own, and failure is always easier to bear if it's someone else's. With the passage of years, optimism either becomes ingrained or exploded, and the best way to sustain it is to remind yourself of past successes and convince yourself it doesn't matter too much if you (temporarily) fail. Mature optimists always have something to look forward to, think of the best things that can happen rather than the worst, try not to worry about things they can do nothing about, and are wounded by suggestions that their habitual expression is a self-satisfied smirk. We would like everyone to share our generally sunny view of the world, but accept, reluctantly, that some grumpy souls are just too old to change.

Orgasm can still occur at our age, and is very nice, too, but let's face it, there are few things more orgasmic at our time of life than having the wax flushed out of your ears, and we can't even do that too often without risking damage.

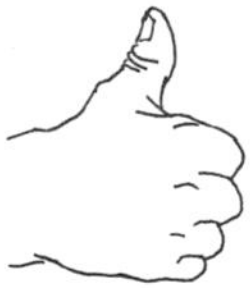

P

Pacemakers are wonderful gadgets for maintaining a regular heartbeat. My mother had one fitted in her late eighties, after she complained of feeling breathless and lacking energy, and it certainly kept her going with minimum fuss. She went in once a year for a tune-up and to have the battery checked. When she passed 101 it became too much of a hassle to take her to the hospital for routine maintenance, and the pacemaker was just left to do its stuff. Which it did so effectively that it prolonged her existence well beyond the point when she could enjoy some quality of life. She frequently said she wanted to "wake up dead," but as the pacemaker could not be turned off or removed without surgery, she had to endure several months of twilight before dying at 103. She enjoyed many years of lively activity thanks to the pacemaker, for which we were all sincerely grateful, but as a supporter of dignity in dying I hope that if I have one fitted it will include an "off" switch so I can slip away peacefully when my time is up.

Paranoia can get more acute when you grow older, especially if you spend a lot of time alone. You worry if the phone doesn't ring, because it means no one cares about you; you worry if it does, because it's bound to be bad news. You're anxious about going out, in case you're late or let your host down or can't get back at a reasonable time; you're anxious about staying in, in case you fall or a start a fire, or might confront a burglar. You know these fears are mostly groundless and could be dissipated if you talked, or even joked, about them, but you don't want to burden others with your anxieties or have them think you're silly. You're very aware that you need to distract yourself by doing more, but when you're paranoid you feel like the kid nobody wants on their team, only half a century older and even more sensitive. You need help. Somewhere there's someone with a hand outstretched to help you over that imagined ring of broken glass that's making you so nervous. The first step's the hardest.

Parents: If you still have yours, congratulations and commiserations. You love them, they drive you demented, and you swear you will never make your grown-up children feel guilty for not visiting more often or, worse, slap them down like errant teenagers when the poor kids were just trying to be helpful. The safest thing we can do as parents is to take the blame for everything. At least we can then act modestly amazed when we're held up as an example.

Passion continues to smolder regardless of age, and though there's often more smoke than flame, it can be kindled without warning by a memory, an encounter, a taste, or a piece of music. What's marvelous, and unsettling, about it is that you get carried away by a sudden emotional rush that leaves you bobbing beyond your comfort zone. It's more than liking, more, even, than loving; it temporarily eclipses everything else, you are dazzled and a little dazed, you can't see straight, you don't act normally, you want only the object of your passion, whether a thing or a person, and while you are gripped absolutely nothing else matters. And then, like a dog that plunges into a muddy pool despite everyone shouting that it shouldn't, you emerge, you shake yourself, and wonder what the fuss was about. You would think we are too old and sensible to allow ourselves such passionate distractions. Fortunately, perhaps, they don't happen that often.

Passwords should only be kept secret from outsiders. Write them down, keep them somewhere safe, and make sure those who will take charge of your affairs when you die know where they are and what they're for. The same is true of advance directives on how you want to be treated if you develop a condition that denies you any quality of life. Sort this out now, when you're still up and running, otherwise your loved ones will have enormous difficulty in accessing your computer to learn what you want them to do, and your bank and savings accounts to pay for it. If you don't, they'll be frustrated and furious instead of impressed and gratified, and your funeral will be miserable. Not that you'll care, but they will.

Patience doesn't miraculously appear when you're old, unlike hair in surprising places. If you haven't developed patience by now, the chances are you never will. You're going to go on fuming when you're stuck behind some even older person fumbling for change at the checkout, or when you've been hanging on the phone for ten minutes only to be told "your call is important to us and one of our operators will be with you shortly." You can be patient with babies and people who simply don't understand what they're being told, because they can't help themselves. With everyone else, you give them a fair chance and if they don't get it, forget it. Life's too short.

Being **patronized** is unforgivable as well as unavoidable. Though we seniors are everywhere, and growing more numerous all the time, the people who keep things running, whether in government, business, transport, or entertainment, are younger than we are, and though many of them are marvelous, there are always some who treat us with barely contained irritation, as if it were our fault they can't give us the answers we want. Like we did, they never think they're going to end up like us, and maybe they secretly resent the way we clutter up shops and operating rooms, or trains and ticket booths, gallivanting around with all the time in the world, and enjoying retirement to boot. We should try not to sink to their level and patronize them back, though it wouldn't take much effort. If we don't always succeed, let's not worry about it.

Pedantry is a tedious insistence on accuracy and should be firmly resisted, because it's so easy for someone you've corrected to check the facts, and you will look like a total jackass if it turns out you were wrong.

The **penis** is an unreliable appendage despite providing many years of pleasure and relief. The main things that go wrong with it are failing to rise to the occasion and making it difficult to pee. Both these problems can be alleviated with medical help, which is some consolation, as is the fact that size no longer matters, if it ever did. *See also Gravity.*

Perseverance is a quality that has gotten us where we are, but it wears thin with age. It's so easy to give up on a task if things go wrong, and it's always tempting to hide doubt and fear of failure behind the belief that there are times when the omens are against us, and we just have to wait until they improve. Our impatience can be all-pervasive, but perseverance is a measure of our continuing engagement with a world that constantly tries to thwart us, especially in petty matters.

Pessimism may be inherited, but is usually the result of a dismal childhood. Where a realist tries to see things as they are, a pessimist is convinced they will end badly, and though they are sometimes surprised and delighted by a happy outcome, they take a gloomy satisfaction in being proved right.

Their low expectations often bring about the result they feared, creating a circle of despair that is hard to escape, and it is difficult to persuade them to take evasive action, such as therapy, because they are convinced it will do no good. Like depression (p. 53), pessimism is miserable to live with, for the victim as well as those around them, as it often results in a narrowing of choices that leads to isolation. The optimist always hopes the sufferer will see there is much to live for and take pleasure in their surroundings, and of course pessimists aren't permanently sunk in gloom. But as the remedy lies in their hands alone, much patience (p. 143) is required, and at our age there isn't an infinite supply of it.

Pets give you unqualified love (whenever you want it if they're dogs, when they feel like it if they're cats) and, provided you feed them regularly, will also forgive you for outbursts of anger, if they're the only one you can take it out on. They're expensive (insurance is advisable) and a bind—you can stay out late and only receive a look of reproach, but a quick foreign trip involves either getting them a pet passport or costly boarding fees. Dogs need a regular walk, which is good exercise, even though they go for the wettest and smelliest patches of ground and, unless you dry them thoroughly, leave hair and muddy paw prints all over your nice clean floor and furniture. On the other hand, they are always available for a hug and a tickle, and if you're on your own they provide a warm furry bed companion that snores just like a partner.

Pleasure:
Giving it as well as getting it matters as much now as it did in our more energetic youth, but you may have to be more inventive, as relying on the old tricks and routines that have become part of your repertoire may no longer be fit for purpose. I'm talking about cooking—what did you think?

Podiatry,
which used to be called chiropody until we Brits adopted the American term for foot doctor, enters our lives when cutting or trimming our toenails becomes a serious challenge. This happens for a variety of reasons: shortness of breath when bending over, difficulties balancing on one leg, increasing girth making it hard to see what's going on below, or a benign tremor (p. 194), which makes getting to grips with sharp scissors or clippers a hazardous and possibly bloody business, especially as the nails themselves seem to grow thicker and tougher with age. You know you're

getting old when you have to call somebody in to do something you've always done for yourself, and having a stranger fiddle with your bare feet is a peculiarly personal invasion of your private parts, but comfort yourself with the thought that it's no more intimate than having your hairdresser attack the top of your head, and it's done in private rather than public.

Politeness is surely ingrained in us and oozes out regardless of any provocation to be rude. It involves taking people seriously, listening to them, and responding courteously. Nothing infuriates a young hooligan more than being treated politely, though that may lead to violence rather than an improvement in manners. When I receive cold calls just when I'm eating or watching TV, I always preface my coldly furious response with "Sorry, but . . ."

In an argument, the thrust of the knife is made all the more effective when delivered politely, and if it makes us look quaintly old-fashioned, or even faintly ridiculous, at least we won't be ignored.

Political correctness is a distorted image of politeness (p. 148), and however absurd some of the linguistic contortions are that people go through to avoid giving offense, we have to pay it lip service. Of course, it's hard to keep up with changes in vocabulary when words we used without thinking are suddenly taboo. Authors who were popular in our parents' day use terms like "Hebrews" or "bolshies" or the N-word, and apologists excuse them on the grounds that they were just reflecting the culture of their time. But those authors were actually anti-Semites, conservatives, and white supremacists, whereas when tolerant and fair-minded people like us employ words that are politically incorrect we never intended to offend anyone. Nevertheless, it's worth trying to come to terms with new terminology, as new words encapsulate new attitudes, and that can sometimes be a sign of progress, or the opposite.

Politics *See Understanding.*

Pornography is so widely available on the internet that I'm sure every man with access to a computer has looked at it more than once. And many women, too, though they usually have better things to do with their time. Being aroused by watching other people who appear to enjoy what they're doing doesn't seem perverted to me, unless what you're watching

is against the law or involves coercion. If you're in a relationship, it may be considered an act of notional infidelity, though it could also be described as a flirtation with fluids that are better out than in. We all know pornography is an industry that has criminal elements and that commodifies and commercializes sex and especially women. It also gives young people an unreal image of what sex is actually like for ordinary people, those who don't have unfeasibly large breasts or huge penises. But the internet offers good stuff as well as bad, and if old people want to pleasure themselves in private watching others do the same, it surely doesn't deserve condemnation out of hand. *See also Masturbation.*

Posture matters only when you catch sight of yourself in a mirror or shop window and wonder who that poor bent old creature is. We've gotten so used to the way we walk, stand, and sit that we imagine our heads are up, our backs straight and our shoulders square, whereas to the rest of the world we resemble an ambling turtle. We know perfectly well that slumping and slouching aren't attractive, make us look small, and enhance the unsightly bulges between our shoulders and our knees. We also know that it's really not hard to make the effort to stand tall and sit straight; what's hard is keeping it up for more than a minute or two. There's no evidence that slouching is bad for your health—I had an uncle by marriage who was a professor of anatomy and insisted that trying to keep the spine rigidly straight was unnatural as well as injurious—and your friends and loved ones are accustomed to the way you look and would be suspicious or alarmed if you suddenly started sitting straight-backed on the edge of the sofa like a Victorian dowager. Some elderly men throw back their shoulders in the presence of an attractive young person, but we all know wit and wisdom are far more enticing than military posture that can't possibly be sustained.

Power, for everyone except monarchs and dictators, is something we *used* to have. In the physical sense, we can't lift or carry what we once did; and the power to command others to do our bidding has long since passed into younger hands. We may carry out traditional roles in our families, or enjoy ceremonial titles in the business we created or expanded, but being addressed as chairman when strategy is decided by the chief executive is like putting a crown on a snowman: It looks impressive, but no one takes it seriously. We are playing a part with which we, and our audience, are wearily familiar, and there's no scope to enlarge it. When the horizon is no longer within reach, you can accept it gracefully (which, unless you are saintly, will scarcely camouflage your resentment); you can bellow defiance (which will result in a lot of eye-rolling exasperation); or you can focus on smaller kingdoms over which you will rule undisputed. Put the skills and experience you have acquired over the years to unexpected use. Small is even more beautiful when you can't see as far as you once could.

Prejudices are what other people have, because they're not as open-minded, rational, tolerant, generous, educated, civilized, wise, balanced, and experienced as we are. It's hard to persuade a prejudiced person to change their mind in private; in public it's impossible, and sometimes dangerous. We have learned over the years to pick the battles we think we can win, but sometimes we have to stand up and fight prejudice even though we will probably be defeated. The scars are honorable, and with any luck we will have inflicted enough damage to make them think again. Or at least reassure ourselves that our instinct for decency is not entirely dormant.

Pretending starts in childhood, and we get better at it as we grow older. But whereas children can change roles swiftly, and are quick to correct anyone who isn't playing their part properly, some of us find it increasingly hard to abandon a character we have pretended to be for so long. It's fine when you act brave to reassure someone who is frightened, or pretend to know more about a subject than you do in order to impress or win an argument—we all do that. It's when you project fantasy as reality—if, say, you pretend to be rich, or organized, when the truth is you are only just managing and your affairs are in chaos—that the danger lies. The chances are you won't be found out if you've carried off the pretense for so many years, but if your mask slips— if, for example, you were taken ill and someone investigated your true situation—you risk your entire reputation being exploded. It doesn't take much for people envious of the character you've created to label you a fantasist, and that could undermine the genuine achievements you may have made. Pretense is addictive, and it requires real resolution to be honest about it before it's too late.

Pride is a virtue, not a vice, and we have surely earned the right to enjoy it. We are proud of what our children and grandchildren achieve, as well as the successes of our friends, provided they are balanced by the occasional failure. Why shouldn't we be proud of our own achievements, or at any rate the ones that were honorably earned, or where the dishonor has been forgotten or forgiven?

Principles: Do these change as we acquire experience and wisdom? Of course they freaking do! There is a subtle difference between principles and convictions: The latter are what we believe about a particular topic, the former a set of beliefs that cover our entire behavior. Convictions can, or should, be changed by facts—if not, they become prejudices (p. 152). Principles are formed by, or in reaction to, education and example, and they alter as we learn more, largely from those we love or live with. If principled behavior is not changed by new experiences, we would never evolve and instead become the grumpy old persons of caricature. As for being models of consistency, where's the fun in that? Keeping ourselves as well as others on their toes is what aging is all about.

Psychotherapy is big business and, like other

big businesses, not always well regulated. There are professional associations for almost every activity, but having a diploma from them is not necessarily a guarantee of respectability. Yet just having somebody listen to you sympathetically is valuable, and if they encourage you to wrap words around your problems, you're on the road to coping with them. You don't have to agree with their analysis of what caused you to despair any more than you have to go back to a physical therapist whose manipulations made you feel worse. And though everyone you know will recommend their favorite, you know you'll go with the friend whose judgment you trust and respect.

Punctuality is a habit that's hard to break.

Whether you're the infuriating type who always leaves time for emergencies, or the sort who still arrives puffing and red-faced and blaming everything but yourself for being late, that's how you've always been, and you're unlikely to change now. I hate keeping people waiting but hate even more being kept waiting and wasting what remains of my time. As a result, I constantly hover between anger and anxiety. If I'm the guest, I think it's only polite to arrive slightly late, as if I'm the host my ambition is to be there slightly ahead of time and appear totally serene and unruffled. You'd think that at our age we'd have stopped worrying about such trivialities, but it's been drummed into us that punctuality is the politeness of kings, and we either conform or rebel.

Quarrels are exhausting and unprofitable between long-term partners, especially when they go over ground that has been dug up as often as a vegetable patch. Between new partners, on the other hand, quarrels can be revealing and informative, as each stakes out ground unfamiliar to the other, and gives them a flash of the weaponry deployed against them. It's a mistake to think you can pick your quarrels, rather, they pick you, and you have to decide whether you're going to sort them out through rational discussion, ignore them and sulk, or blow on them until they flare into open warfare. If you join battle, it becomes a matter of victory or defeat, though a master of strategy should be able to persuade their opponent to surrender by making them believe they have won.

Questions should be answered seriously when they come from our grandchildren, though of course we are entitled, indeed expected, to embroider the truth. We can also be open when questioned by people who appear genuinely interested in our opinions and history, for which of us does not enjoy the opportunity to talk about ourselves? Where we should be guarded, however, is when asked questions that we know will be stored and sold as marketing data. We live in a society that wants to know so much about us, their questions amount to an invasion of privacy. I don't mind ticking or filling in boxes with my name, address, and date of birth in order to open an account or make a purchase, but as that should give them enough to establish my bona fides, I don't see why I should tell them where I was born, my marital state, or how I came across their services. The trouble is, they probably know these things anyway, as few of us think the answers we too readily supply will be used against us. We also tend to believe that with so much information available, the chances of us being singled out for some malign purpose are as slim as winning the lottery. We could be wrong.

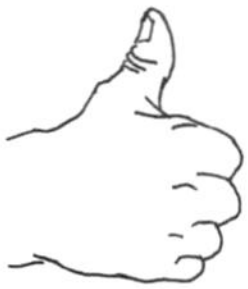

R

Realism is important at our age, but we shouldn't
let it cramp our imagination entirely. We haven't
gotten this far without being realistic about what does
and doesn't work, and we know our limitations as
well as those of the people we interact with. But being
hardened by experience needn't stop us from taking
on a challenge. Optimists will believe they'll emerge
triumphant and pessimists will expect disaster, but even
the most realistic of us still has dreams.

Regrets are like the stuffed toys we comforted
ourselves with as children, things we should have grown
out of but can't bear to throw away. We all have much

to regret, so many encounters that ended badly, the memories of which make us sit up in the middle of the night with a nightmare shudder, either because we're still owed an apology, or we didn't apologize when we could and should have. We know we shouldn't dwell on these matters, but like all the stuff we've stored out of sight, they're never quite out of mind. Of course we should have a good clean-out and face the future cleansed, but who wants to be clean and pure when the rest of the world fights dirty? However ashamed we are of the things we regret, like that scruffy old toy, it's a comfort to know we can give them a private airing when we need to.

Relaxing is hard when you're as busy as we are, latecomers to a culture that insists on instant response as well as instant gratification. To relax properly is not the same as wasting time (p. 206)—you have to be disciplined, which appears to be a contradiction in terms. You need to set aside a period of at least twenty minutes during which you use whatever method you prefer to empty your mind and allow your body to find its natural alignment. I know that sounds like psychobabble, and I'm not good about meditation (p. 123), nor have I tried yoga (p. 213), but I did find

the Alexander Technique—a method of relaxation
originally developed for actors with stage fright—to
be effective in easing aches and pains, and it has the
additional benefit of making me less dependent on
an inhaler for allergies by teaching me how to relax
my chest and lungs. It didn't make me taller or more
attractive, but then relaxing is about looking inward
and disengaging from the usual concerns that absorb
our energies and nag at our confidence.

Religion is a subject on which people of our age
have long ago made up our minds. As a Jewish atheist
all I'm going to say is that the rituals for solemn events
like weddings and funerals still bring people together
for a common purpose, whatever their faith, and
that places of worship are impressive monuments to
community belief. At its best, religion offers charity to
the poor, care for the sick, and comfort to the lonely; at
less than its best it cloaks in respectability the small-
minded, the censorious, the intolerant, and the fanatic.
But while a secular or humanist ceremony can equal
the religious ones in emotional grandeur, they don't
have the hymns, do they?

Resolutions have been broken so often during the many years we've been striving for improvement that it's a wonder we go on making them. It's a combination of habit, optimism, and self-delusion: We find that a favorite garment has suddenly grown too small, and in a fit of self-disgust we resolve to give up our favorite vices, and while we're about it we'll also stop swearing or growling at our loved ones. We end up fulfilling none of those resolutions, and console ourselves by overindulging even more, telling ourselves it doesn't really matter at our time of life, and conveniently ignoring the fact that while we're very good at criticizing a lack of willpower in others, we've learned very little about controlling our own.

Respect should be accorded us for our sheer survival, if not for our achievements. Sadly, we do not always receive our due, because there are now so many of us oldies our age is unremarkable and hardly merits attention. What can we do to gain respect, assuming that's what we want? Heroic deeds are probably beyond us, philanthropy is so common it would have to be on a massive scale, and while a sudden change of behavior would rightly be regarded with suspicion, consistency is too boring to alter attitudes, unless you're royalty. You don't get respect by drawing attention to yourself, or if you do it doesn't last long, and though the ability to make people laugh is much respected, it's no good if you can't deliver a punchline effectively. In my view, respect is like approval and the universal desire to be loved: If you do what you enjoy as well as you can and pretend not to care what other people think, respect may be yours. Or not, but at least you're having fun.

Responsibility can't, alas, be shirked, at least not until we can no longer take responsibility for ourselves. We may frequently want to take a step back, to let others stand in the firing line, to watch from a distance while those we love ignore our advice and do things that end in tears, whether it's dissipating their emotional energy on doomed relationships or wasting their political energy on futile gestures. Of course they should act responsibly, but if they don't, we can't give up on them any more than we can turn up the thermostat and stop worrying about global warming, or pick up a plastic bottle of water and ignore the fact that it will find its way into the deepest and darkest parts of our oceans. We grew up believing the individual can and should make a difference, and just because we've done our part doesn't, sadly, mean there isn't more to be done. However tempting it is to let others carry the torch for progress, the need for effective action is greater than ever, and because we wouldn't be where we are today if we hadn't acted responsibly at least some of the time, we owe it to ourselves to carry on.

Retirement is a nonsensical term: To call yourself "retired" is a totally inaccurate description of all the activities and anxieties that fill your waking, and often your sleeping, hours. Just because you are no longer in full-time employment doesn't mean you have withdrawn from the world, or that you have nothing more to contribute to it. I am self-employed and still working in my seventies; the father of a friend of mine still put in a few hours most days at his desk, and he was 102. Being forced to give up a job you enjoyed just because you have reached an arbitrary age is ridiculous and insulting, and a bus pass and retirement funds are small compensation. If we're still active, capable, and taking pride and pleasure in our work, we should be encouraged to continue.

Retirement villages, unlike retirement
homes, sound quite attractive if you can afford them.
You have your own living space, there are plenty of
leisure activities, communal restaurants for those who
can't be bothered to cook, and assistance and medical
care are always available. The grounds and buildings
are secure, and though your neighbors are strangers
they will be of your generation and suffer from similar
ailments (p. 7). Unlike a retirement home, where the
staff struggle to care for a disparate collection of often
demented people who can't look after themselves, a
retirement village doesn't operate a regime with a
strict set of rules that benefit the owner rather than the
occupant. But would you want to live in a community
consisting only of people like you—people of similar
age, income, and interests? The village we live in had a
properly mixed population when we bought our house,
but thanks to the ridiculous rise in property prices only
the seriously wealthy can now afford to buy here. Isn't
the joy of living in a mixed community having children
around, and young people in touch with the latest
trends, even the occasional vandal to grumble about, as
well as persons with different backgrounds, experiences,
and views that may not be the same as yours? When I

get to the stage of being unable to take care of myself, I hope I'll be able to afford a caregiver and have family around to keep an eye on me and them. If not, I'd opt for assisted dying with dignity, but whatever the case I wouldn't want to live with people just like me: That would be boring, and boredom (p. 26) is what kills you.

Routines are the banisters that get us through the day. They are deeply personal, and often seem ridiculous to outsiders who have their own rituals to keep them going. You probably don't remember how or why you started on your particular routine, and assuming you don't suffer from OCD, you'd regard it as quite flexible and subject to change at whim. Routines offer a comfortable straitjacket in which you can do stuff without having to think about it, but when they start to run your life, rather than you being in charge, they've become obsessions (p. 135), and need to be challenged.

Rudeness has to be instinctive, and is stronger if laced with wit, but if you can't manage that, you can show you're in control by staying calm. If an outburst is unstoppable, let rip and leave, preferably before they can respond.

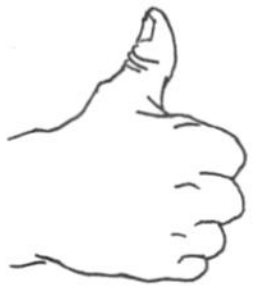

S

Saving is what survivors like us do instinctively. Money aside, we save things we know will come in handy, as well as things that are worth saving just in case they become useful. We can't help ourselves, even though we've vowed to *downsize* (ridiculous word, like something Alice might do in Wonderland), and get rid of all our clutter to make it easier for our children when we've gone. It may be that we are influenced by the example of our grandparents (my grandma scrubbed tinfoil and saved it for reuse) and our parents, who stockpiled everything from toilet paper to canned food long after the war and rationing had ended. And there were no sell-by dates in those days: You kept stuff until it stank, rotted, or, in the case of cans, blew its top. Though our own lives have seen the longest period of peace in Europe ever recorded, we still have the memories of war imprinted on our minds, and part of us wants to hoard stuff in case of disaster. But as our children, benign products of the age of obsolescence, won't touch food that's out of date, our saving is something of a wasted exercise, and they covertly or openly mock us for it. Unlike their attitude to our saving money . . .

Secrets are not all that safe when we grow forgetful about who we're not supposed to share them with. I'm not known for my discretion, but I can still persuade friends to tell me their secrets, because at our age gossip is as highly prized as when we were at school. There are few things more thrilling than betraying a confidence and knowing it will in turn be betrayed: It's not necessarily malicious but more like a game of hot potato where you want to get rid of the goods to avoid paying a penalty. Of course, if someone younger confides in you and swears you to secrecy, you have to honor your vow, though if you suspect they might harm themselves, or others, you should

be devious enough to warn those who can prevent
that happening, and then protest your innocence to
the one you have betrayed. They won't believe you,
but it's better than saying you did it for their own
good, and they might even be grateful, or you can so
comfort yourself. As for our contemporaries, after a
glass or two most of them are ready to spill the beans
to anyone within hearing, but as the whole point of
having secrets is sharing them when you shouldn't,
who can blame them, especially when we'd do the
same? *See also Betrayal.*

Self-employment is for those of us who are
too bullheaded to work for someone else, and who have
the energy, confidence, and communication skills to
persuade people to use our services. As we still (I trust)
have much to offer, we can either use our knowledge
and expertise to become consultants, or we can become
entrepreneurs (p. 66) and find a gap in the market to do
something that nobody else is doing or, if they are, do it
better. It's risky, of course, and you have to work harder
than you ever did for some company or corporation,
and make all the important decisions as well as take
responsibility for anyone you employ. But no one
can fire you, unless you do something illegal or go

bankrupt, and if you've gotten it right, which with all your experience you freaking well should have, you'll wake up each morning looking forward to the next challenge. Or at least with a list (p. 116) of things that'll keep you busy.

Selfishness at our age is a way of surviving, and may also be a protection against being let down after an embittering experience. You don't get to be seriously old without looking out for yourself, unless you're a saint, and if you've reached that enviable point when you don't really care what other people think, putting yourself first comes naturally. Ideally you shouldn't cultivate selfishness to the point when no one else will come near or care for you, unless they're being paid, but it's perfectly possible to combine being selfish with judicious generosity that will encourage others to do what you want, and even love you for it.

Sex slows from a fiery tango to a stately waltz. I have never quite believed those men who say they are relieved to have reached the age when they no longer feel the sexual urge, which someone compared to being unchained from a devouring monster. Most people don't stop thinking about sex when they grow older, they just don't do it as often. That's surely not because we lack the opportunity, since most of us no longer work full time. It's because at our age consensual sex requires tact and diplomacy, and if penetrative sex is the objective, there is the real possibility of failure. Men tend to bury memories of coital catastrophe, but past disasters loom large when the equipment fails to respond to the urgent demand of its owner. Like accusatory ghosts, they can turn haunt into humiliation, which can only be banished by medical help or, better, a sense of humor. Of course, sex at our age needn't involve penetration. A good cuddle can work wonders if the partners have the time, patience, and desire to please one another. And there's still time to learn something new, provided you're prepared to put aside years of reticence and actually talk about what gives each of you pleasure. Though aging bodies slapping against each other can seem faintly ridiculous, conversation can turn embarrassment and frustration into an enjoyable experience. The most active organ in the body—apart from the heart and brain—is, after all, the tongue.

Sexism has no place in our culture or society, and those who abused their power to force themselves on people who wanted nothing to do with them sexually have lived to regret it. This isn't political correctness (p. 148), it's learning from experience, and though we weren't perfect, nor were most of us exploitative monsters. We who matured in the 1960s tried to behave like good guys, and if we can't modify behavior that is now deemed inappropriate and treat people of different genders with the respect we expect ourselves, we've made no progress and should be ashamed of ourselves.

Shopping can be a treat as long as you can afford it, but people divide into those who look for something particular, and those who go shopping not knowing exactly what they want, except they know they want something. And there's division over the technology, of course: Shopping online is so easy once you get the hang of it, I'm amazed anyone wants to spend their time and money getting to an overcrowded shop on overcrowded roads and then wasting hours dithering over what to buy, squeezing the fruit and sniffing the veg, when you can return stuff bought online if it's not to your liking. Even going into a bookshop, which naturally I support and encourage others to do, renders me brain-dead within minutes because I'm overwhelmed by choice. Of course I recognize the social value of going shopping, and though I can usually think of things I'd rather do, my curmudgeonly attitude always vanishes when I meet someone I can gossip with rather than trudging the aisles.

Sighing is something we do far too much of. We sigh when we sink into our chair and when we get out of it, when we bend over to take off our clothes and when we struggle to put them on, when we get into bed, walk around the shops, prepare a meal, or do the dishes. It's not like puffing when you've walked up a bit of a hill, or having to take a rest because you've overexerted yourself, it's not a grunt of pain or a squeak of surprise—our sighing has become a reflex, a soft and comforting exhalation that we hardly notice. It makes us sound as if we're sorry for ourselves and bearing great burdens with noble fortitude, and we should really tell ourselves to stop it.

Singing is one of the most enjoyable ways of showing off in public, and if you're not very good at it no one will know, apart from the people on either side of you. As a leisure pursuit it is good for posture (you have to stand straight in order to let your diaphragm swell), the lungs (you have to expand them fully and breathe properly), and the brain (whether or not you can read music, you have to work out where the tune is going and how your part fits in with the others). It's sociable—a good leader or teacher attracts singers from all over the place; it gets you out of the house and helps combat stress by making you concentrate on producing a lovely noise to the exclusion of all else; when it works it's an incredibly satisfying achievement to which you all contributed; and if you're really eager, you and your group can give a little concert for an audience who may be even older than you are. And unlike a book group (p. 25), you don't have to do homework unless you can't resist practicing when you're alone.

Size matters, even at our age. Not your chest or your penis, but the bit in between, for starters: If it's pear-shaped you attempt to disguise it, if it contracts you worry you've got cancer. Those of us who aren't tall should have given up worrying about our height years ago, but as we all shrink as we grow older, people who haven't seen us for a while may think we're disappearing altogether. When it comes to possessions, if once we were concerned about having a bigger house/car/garden than our neighbors, now we fret over whether their largeness is too much for us to cope with. At least size is irrelevant where conversation—the glue that holds us all together—is concerned: The tongue is one of the most active organs in our bodies and, like our hands, feet, and head, its size never alters.

Skin is amazing at restoring itself, but bruises, grazes, cuts, and wounds seem to take forever to heal at our age, even if you are accustomed to keeping yourself elastic with moisturizer (p. 127). The unblemished sheen of youth becomes mottled with moles, warts, lumps, bumps, freckles, and liver spots; hairs sprout in places you don't want them and cease to grow in places you do; and the veins that used to lie delicately beneath the surface now make themselves as obvious as knotted string. Lines, creases, wrinkles, and furrows are all evidence of use or abuse, and while skin is marvelously accommodating when it comes to containing the parts that swell, it also sags and flakes and droops and forms folds that become tricky to clean. Of course if you can afford it you can have your blemishes sliced off, your hairs stripped, your wrinkles smoothed, and your saggy parts tightened or plumped up, but our skin is the living and inescapable testament to everything our bodies have experienced, and we should be proud of it in all its flawed but marvelous cragginess.

Sleep *See Insomnia.*

Snoring is one of the few things that inspire murderous thoughts in otherwise stable couples. Both genders snore at our age and both protest that they don't; men may snore more loudly than women, mainly when they're drunk, but they stop—temporarily, at least—when prodded or shouted at, or they wake up with a resentful "Whatsamatter?" and, infuriatingly, fall asleep again. My wife mutters "Sorry" when I bounce on the mattress to stop her snoring, and of course I would also apologize if I believed I was really disturbing her, though the noise is obviously made by her or the Snore Fairy. There is no effective cure other than separate bedrooms, if you can afford them. And you can always come together for a healing cuddle.

Solitude, as opposed to loneliness (p. 117), is an admirable demonstration of character and self-sufficiency. I'd like to think I could manage it if I had to, but I suspect I'd fail. Solitude means enjoying

your own company, keeping yourself entertained and stimulated, being responsible for your own actions, and not caring if you don't see another soul. If you've been in a relationship and are suddenly bereaved, you may withdraw into solitude to come to terms with your grief, or escape the well-wishers who, however well intentioned, won't leave you alone. If you've never been, or had the chance to be, solitary, it's an opportunity to try something punishingly different, knowing (if you don't leave it too long) the world will welcome your return. If you take to it, it's fine until you fall or get ill or incapacitated, and though you might be able to rely on social services, it could be difficult to readjust to the proximity of other human beings. But there is something noble and antique and ascetic about choosing solitude in a world so inextricably interconnected. You just need an inner strength not all of us possess—certainly not me.

Sports *See Games.*

Stinginess creeps up on us unpredictably and
makes us stubbornly refuse to open our wallets or flash
our credit cards, the way a horse will inexplicably
refuse to jump a fence. It's not an act of prudence,
like saving (p. 171), it's an atypical fit of miserliness,
usually provoked by outrageous prices or demands that
are suddenly too much to bear. We think of it as an
individual act of rebellion against crass commercialism;
others will view it as mere meanness. They may shake
their heads, but they will probably follow our example.

Stoicism, or fortitude in the face of misfortune,
is a front we keep up for the sake of our friends and
family. But while no one likes jeopardizing a reputation
for strength by crumbling in a moment of weakness,
there are times when we need to show that we are still
capable of being scared or overcome by emotion. We
need it for ourselves, because being brave all the time
is too hard, and quite boring, and others need to know
we're not superhuman. Or not always.

Suicide: When I was young, I thought anyone who talked about killing themselves was just seeking attention. I was wrong, several times over. Now people of our generation talk openly about suicide when they are desperately ill and have no quality of life. They don't want to be a burden to those around them, and seek an end to their suffering. The law in most states is currently against them, but that might change. I support dignity in dying, but I learned a lesson from neighbors who told us—and their children and anyone who was interested—that they would commit suicide before they became incapable of looking after themselves. They'd been scarred by having to care for their own parents and were resolved not to hamper their children's lives. At the time, we all thought they were acting from the noblest of motives and willingly witnessed their signatures on a declaration of intent that attested they were of sound mind. We and their children were in our thirties, they were in their early sixties, and we never thought they'd do it. But they did, a few years later, and far from admiring their resolve, we and their families were stricken with grief, guilt, and fury. Instead of respecting their selfless sacrifice, it was perceived as a gesture of pure selfishness. They were perfectly fit, and unlike the suicide of someone for whom life is unbearable, our neighbors' deaths seemed like a ridiculous waste. As it usually does, to those left behind.

Superstitions stay with even the most

skeptical of us. I don't mean knocking on wood when talking about how healthy we feel, I mean those little hangovers from our childhood like not opening an umbrella indoors or walking under ladders. We invent new superstitions, too—one of mine is that if I get to a certain point on my daily walk without being passed by a car, I'll have good news from a publisher. This may have happened once, and crystallized into a superstition because I wanted it to happen again, but of course it's pure wishful thinking, as well as an attempt to insure against disaster. It's also a belief, diluted almost to invisibility like homeopathic medicine, in things beyond our understanding: We're a superstitious species and we keep our fingers crossed.

Surprise sustains a relationship, and can also

destroy it. You can do something unexpected for your partner that makes them realize how joyful and generous you are; you can do something unexpected to your partner that shows you're an unreliable shit. Without surprise there's boredom (p. 26), and we all know how fatal that is; with surprise come consequences, the unpredictability of which can itself be surprising. But life's a gamble, and at our age who can resist a flutter?

Survival is hard to live with if all your contemporaries have died or moved to Australia, and infinitely harder if you've survived the death of a child or younger friend. You struggle to carry on, you wonder if it's worth it, even though we're all being threatened with longer, healthier lives. You grieve, and you get over your grief, because that's what survival involves, and if you survive long enough you become someone people congratulate, even venerate, not just because of your age, but because of your history. Our parents went through the losses of one or two world wars and survived, most of them with less psychological damage than seventy years of peace has inflicted on us. Survival is something to celebrate, providing it gives you more pleasure than pain. At least you don't need advice on how to survive, because you've managed perfectly well without it.

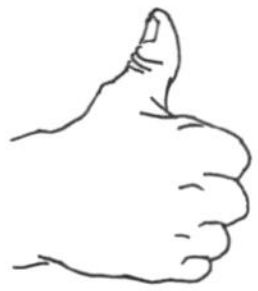

T

Tactlessness is something older people are good at because we don't worry much about the consequences. It's usually an impulsive expression of a view you simply can't keep to yourself— like my grandmother, who after watching me proudly change our daughter's diaper, said "He's put it on so tight the poor child can't break wind!" The undeniable truth of the observation gains you admiration (though not from the wounded victim) as someone who is fearlessly outspoken. Tactlessness isn't planned, and you can always defend yourself against a charge of being outrageously rude with the line "Did I really say that? I never meant to," as if your mouth opened all by itself.

Targets are acceptable when you set them yourself, as opposed to those pointless and useless goals imposed by ignorant interfering know-it-alls. We all need something to make it worth getting up in the morning, and the trick is to aim to do something that will make a difference, if only to you, whether it's walking a little farther, a little faster, or resisting the temptation to have a second helping. Some masochists like to announce their target, challenging friends and family to hold them to it, and upbraid them if they fail; those who are more self-contained keep their targets to themselves, avoiding humiliation should they falter, and enjoying private self-congratulation—which can of course be discreetly shared—when they succeed. *See also Ambition.*

Tasks *See Chores.*

Taste can set like concrete once you've passed your middle years, and only the explosive effect of a catalytic experience or a new lover will make you look at things differently. We know what we like from quite early in adulthood, and our taste is formed by our desire to impress the people we respect, by our need to be different from our parents, and by what we can afford. But in maturity, where food is concerned our taste becomes limited to what's on offer; in clothes it comes down to what's comfortable; in decoration, whatever we can live with is preferable to the tedium of calling in painters; and in books, pictures, or records—we've collected so much we're more interested in filling gaps than acquiring anything new. That is, until that seismic moment when we are suddenly fed up with everything around us and want to throw it all out and be somebody different. It may be provoked by bereavement or the need to move to a smaller place or a casual remark that makes us realize we haven't changed anything for decades. Most of us allow the moment to pass; those who don't become as contemptuous as teenagers about people who think their taste never needs refreshing. Inertia vs. upheaval: I'm not taking sides.

Technology is mostly what our grandchildren

handle, as they're the only ones who have the patience to enlighten us dimwits. We're not Luddites: We've lived through so much technological change that has made our lives infinitely easier—the progress from coal or gas fires (or paraffin stoves) to central heating, from crystal set radios to TV on demand, from whistling

kettles to microwaves, from inkwells to computers—
that we are grateful rather than resentful. There are
two things we can object to. One is the "updates"
or techno-crap that could only be of conceivable use
to the nerds who invented it, to show off their nerdy
skills and justify their nerdy salaries, which prompts
the plaintive question: "Why can't they leave things
alone?" The other is the sinister abuse of technology
for political ends, the manipulation of information
to persuade people who think of themselves as quite
savvy to believe fake news. This heavily funded techno-
propaganda employs artificial intelligence, bots, and
algorithms, and even if we're not sure what the hell
that means, we have to be very much on our guard and
keep warning people when they start confusing rhetoric
with reality.

T

Temper at our age is like a dormant volcano: It rumbles rather than flares, but when it erupts, the lava is messy. We know from long experience that exploding in front of our loved ones is counterproductive and is either ignored or creates an atmosphere that results in indigestion and insomnia, especially when it is, as usual, our fault. And a bad-tempered outburst in front of friends merely makes us look petulant and foolish. We may be somewhat more tolerant than when we were younger, and minor irritations have become part of everyday living; throwing a temper tantrum won't change anything, and doesn't even make us feel much better. But just occasionally we lose it, perhaps because of an accumulation of petty irritations, perhaps out of sheer boredom or exasperation because things aren't going quite as we wanted and we're fed up with being asked what's wrong. So we blow, and because we're not used to losing control even we may tremble at the force of it. If you're lucky, your audience will feel your temper is justified; if it surprises them as much as it surprises you, you may lose a friend or be in for a night in the spare room or have the doctors check you over. It's good to know you still have the energy to show your temper, but it's also frightening, for you as well as them. It may be forgiven, but it won't be quickly forgotten. *See also Anger.*

Threats, as we know from bringing up our incredibly well-adjusted children, should never be uttered and then not carried out. If you threaten to withhold payment from a plumber who messed up the installation of your new dishwasher until he's put it right, you've got to stick to your guns, even if he denies responsibility and threatens to call in the cops, which could seriously damage your hitherto impeccable credit rating. We don't issue threats the way we used to when we were younger and cockier, and we've learned that it's usually possible to arrive at a compromise that leaves both sides reasonably satisfied. But from time to time you find yourself in a position where you're being taken advantage of, and you may have to threaten sanctions to show that just because you're old doesn't mean you're a pushover. What you have to ensure is that the threat is within your power to execute. It's no good saying you'll expose their criminal behavior in the media if the only reporter you know retired years ago, or threatening to sue when your lawyer only handles divorces. Threats rumble in when reason has failed, and they should always be proportionate.

Tolerance is important but you don't have to go overboard. You've spent years tolerating your partner's little idiosyncrasies, like cutting their toenails in the bath, but that doesn't mean you have to welcome for dinner the first person they ever slept with, who they re-met on Facebook. You may tolerate your daughter-in-law's reactionary politics, but you don't have to stand for her being mean to your son. With grandchildren, you can tolerate pretty much anything if they're with their parents, and wait until you have them on their own to teach them how to be responsible human beings. As for the rest of the world, I think we've earned the right to be intolerant of mediocrity, knavery, lying, hypocrisy, cruelty, and gross incompetence. We should, if we have the energy and are sufficiently incensed, make clear our dissatisfaction and offer suggestions for improvement, politely if possible, forcefully if not. Being tolerant doesn't mean accepting behavior we find intolerable: Speaking our mind may not make much difference, it may (or may not) make us feel better, but we'd kick ourselves for doing nothing.

Treats are not rewards for good behavior: Those are bribes. Treats are little pleasures that can be given on a whim, without any moralizing about them being earned. No one is too old or too young to enjoy a treat. The joy of it is in the surprise more than the indulgence. Be generous with treats, especially to yourself.

Tremors are disconcerting at best and terrifying at worst. You find your hand shaking when you pour a cup of coffee, or pick up a pen to add something to the shopping list, and you're convinced you've got Parkinson's or MS. But as the doctors will tell you, tremors are a common occurrence as we grow older, often being a benign palsy that has no obvious cause—switching from ordinary to decaffeinated coffee makes little difference—and no serious effect on your general health. You may drop or spill things, and people will notice as you fill up their glasses, but unless you've ruined their clothes they should be too polite to say anything, as they will realize it's just another annoying infirmity we seniors have to live with.

Trust is something we have to rely on more and more as we get older and shakier. We've learned enough over the years to know whom not to trust, and if we can't rely on our family, friends, and advisers to look after us and our affairs when we no longer trust ourselves to do so, it's probably too late to worry. Mind you, that trust has to be earned: My mother kept us all up to the mark and questioned—and criticized—every decision we made on her behalf until she was over 100, when she decided that as we hadn't bankrupted her or put her in a home, she might as well trust us and stop worrying. We might have wished she'd done it earlier, but it was a sweet moment nonetheless.

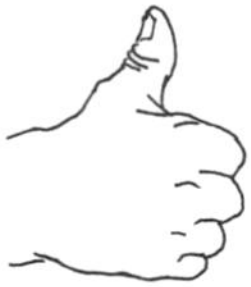

Understanding should be a cinch at our age, given the sympathy we've acquired with experience. It's sometimes hard to understand erratic behavior in our friends—when they split unexpectedly or fly into a sudden rage—but we can ascribe that to frustration or senility. It is far harder to understand the current trend toward a culture that threatens to negate everything we value. I'm not just talking about fashion or language, I mean a political shift as profound and challenging as the one our parents lived through in the 1930s and 1940s, a mood that rejects what we call rationalism, tolerance, multiculturalism, and dialogue in favor of insularity, intolerance, intemperance, and hate. Is this our fault for allowing our 1960s' permissiveness to drift into indifference as politics became increasingly remote from our everyday concerns? We just wanted everyone to be themselves and make a difference, but when that didn't happen in the way we hoped, most of us shrugged and got on with our lives. The young populists blame our generation as well as the baby boomers for fucking everything up, and I completely understand that feeling of fierce joy people get when someone successfully challenges our corrupt and complacent rulers. But don't the young understand the consequences of putting illiberal ideas into practice? Have they no feeling for their victims, those marginalized like themselves but of a different color or culture? It's easy for us to sigh and say what comes around goes around, because we may not be around to see civilization growing foul. We have to engage with those who attack our so-called liberal attitudes, and make them understand that, for all its faults, representative democracy delivers more benefits to more people than a cruel, lying, ferociously corrupt autocracy. A world without the values we've lived by won't be worth living in, even if we're not here to see it.

Upbringing still seems to matter, even though our own is past mending. When a child, grandchild, or friend brings someone around for your approval, you can immediately tell what kind of upbringing they've had. Though you wouldn't dream of commenting on it, unless confident they can withstand your candor, it's hard to overcome doubts if the qualities you value— manners, respect, modesty—are missing. But if you breathe a word of criticism you will immediately be accused of snobbery, and even if you try to put things right by citing examples of people with different upbringings getting along well, you will be attacked for your old-fashioned views on class distinctions. We fight our upbringing until we are confident enough to accept it, and if you've been brought up properly you should leave it at that.

Vanity keeps us going. When we stop caring how we look, how we entertain, how we choose to impress our friends and enemies, or how we spend our money, we might as well be dead. Far from being a vice, the daily struggle to keep up appearances motivates us all. It's only when it becomes an obsession that crowds out everything else, such as a sense of proportion, that it becomes dangerous.

Vegetarians don't necessarily lose weight or live longer, but becoming one, especially in your maturity, is a way of surprising your friends and family, challenging chefs to come up with something interesting (the French and Russians are disappointing as well as disappointed), and also involves the sort of compromises that are so much a part of growing older. I surprised my teenage daughters by turning vegetarian after I had plucked, gutted, cooked, and eaten a pheasant shot by a friend—not because I was squeamish, but because I could no longer condone the killing of such a beautiful bird, after which it was easy to give up eating anything with a face. But I still enjoy eggs, love cheese, drink milk, and wear leather shoes, though I tell myself they come from cows that lived to a peaceful old age, preferably in a socialist country. It's not a religion or a fad; it's a lifestyle that just happens to benefit the environment, and one that makes us feel better—not necessarily superior—about ourselves and the world.

Vitamins are either essential to keep us healthy at our age, or an expensive rip-off and complete waste of time, depending on whom you believe. Despite endorsements from wrinkled celebrities of the benefits they derive from taking the damn things, if we've gotten this far, surely the diet we've followed for years supplies all our needs? And as a member of that generation who were force-fed vitamins when rationing was in force—in England we all remember that sweetened orange juice, cod liver oil, and that syrupy yeasty stuff that came in a brown bottle—I rebel against taking further vitamins on principle.

Vocabulary changes so rapidly there's little point in our trying to keep up with it. We're perfectly capable of holding a decent conversation with the words we've acquired over the years, and as with technology (p. 189), if we attempt to use the new slang we're bound to get it wrong and become objects of pity bordering on contempt. Apart from political correctness (p. 148), the neologisms the young use are so ugly and limited in application, they're better avoided. The language we learned is expressive, flexible, and often beautiful, and though of course it's always in a state of flux, if it's properly used it will be properly appreciated. Amirite?

Vulnerability is not limited to those who can't take proper care of themselves. Even the strongest and most outwardly successful of us is wounded by a hurtful comment, whether or not it was maliciously meant, and though we have developed a thick skin over the years, we still bleed inside, like we did as teenagers. When in pain, we tend to forget that the young are even more vulnerable than we are—they haven't had our experience and are still working out their survival strategies. So don't lash out unless you can't stop yourself, and if you do let fly, be ready with comfort.

Walking is the cheapest and simplest form of exercise (p. 69), assuming you're capable of putting one foot in front of the other. You don't need any special equipment or skills, you can go wherever you like at whatever speed suits your mood. The experts say it should be fast enough to raise your heartbeat, yet not too fast to hold a conversation, but even ambling for half an hour is going to stretch your limbs and improve your circulation. If you're on your own you can think, if you're in company you can chat—conversation in the open is different from talking inside, perhaps because you focus on things you can see rather than abstract matters. You observe more walking than you

do using any other form of transport; you can stop
when you want to without worrying about parking;
you can extend your distance or your speed if you want
to push yourself; or you can simply stop and admire,
which works especially well with a dog. You won't grow
thin, but your complexion will improve as well as your
fitness, and if you get bored you can always put on
some headphones. I've seen people walking and texting
or having loud conversations on their cell phones, but
at our age walking offers an escape from all that, a
delightful opportunity to be solitary—unless you're
with the dog and bump into a fellow owner.

Wasting time is a practice so frequently
condemned by our parents when we were teenagers that
now we have the leisure to indulge in it, we've forgotten
how, or feel guilty even contemplating it. Which is
ridiculous, as idling, or bumming about doing nothing
in particular, is a valuable antidote to the puritanical
drive to make every second count. We don't want to
descend into sloth, which could quickly become boring
(p. 26), but being moderate in maturity means striking a
balance between activity and relaxation, between ticking
items off our to-do list and taking a couple of hours off
to enjoy something that doesn't have a point. Whether

that's staying in bed on a rainy day watching trashy TV or sneaking off to the bar for no better reason than you fancy a drink, wasting time is like making compost: It's at its most productive just before it turns to sludge.

Well-being has recently become an industry. I'm aware that I'm tiptoeing into it with this book, which I hope will make you feel better about yourself, but I'm not promoting any products, or trying to get you to spend money (apart from the price of the book), and the only advice I offer is to be wary, which you were already. Our well-being depends on the good things we have experienced, like love and laughter, and if you've lost or forgotten those, your instinct, your friends, and your common sense will surely be more effective than anyone who purports to peddle happiness.

Willpower tends to atrophy with age, when vanity loses out to laziness. But it can be defibrillated into action by a chance remark, sometimes by a child, that makes us see ourselves as others do. When our daughter was pregnant with her second child, our young grandson patted my stomach and said, "Baby sleeping?" I went on a diet immediately. It didn't last, but I was shocked into making the effort.

Wills should be regularly updated to take account of changing circumstances, including our own. We should also make those close to us, and our doctors, aware of what treatment we do or don't want if we develop an illness that denies us any quality of life, or if we can no longer make decisions for ourselves. It's another thing we put off, because no one likes to dwell on their own mortality, but some of the beneficiaries you named in your will may have died or forfeited your good opinion, some of the charities you wanted to help may have become mired in scandal or stopped functioning, a divorce or new relationship within the family may mean you want to reward or punish different people from those you originally envisaged. It's your last chance to show your approval in concrete terms, and provided you revise your will when you're relatively calm and relatively sane, you should get on with it.

Work–life balance matters enormously, but if you haven't worked that out by now, it's probably too late. You'll be tempted to tell other people how to organize their lives better, but unless you're a shining example of someone who got it right, they'll ignore you, as they will most advice (p. 5) that wasn't what they asked for.

Worrying is something we're really good at. We're anxious about our families because we know all the bad things that could happen, and we privately worry about ourselves as death and disease diminish our circle. A certain amount of stress is good for keeping the adrenaline flowing, but when it makes you feel ill or inhibits your ability to function, you have to seek help. Sharing your worries is supposed to make you put them in perspective, but your long-term partner may be so familiar with them they dismiss them or offer perfunctory reassurance, while your closest friends may listen only for a gap into which they can insert their own concerns. If you have nobody to talk to about things you feel may sound trivial but which have suddenly assumed alarming importance— your health, your finances, the fact that you haven't heard from someone you were hoping might call—you need a professional, someone who can listen impartially and offer advice objectively. You may think you've managed perfectly well without sharing your weaknesses with strangers, but worrying can be like a disease, and you need all the help you can get.

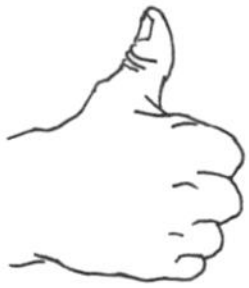

Xenophobia is irrational when a country relies on and has benefited so much from immigrants, and it makes a fool of the comforting idea that better education produces more tolerant citizens. But in our lifetime, immigration has increased as much as inequality, and when people feel they are denied the benefits that others enjoy, the easiest thing is to blame strangers for taking what they think of as rightfully theirs. However, as nobody takes any notice of us when we point out that immigrants are doing the jobs we natives no longer want, we can only hope that if they are shut out, it will not be long before being deprived of their services will become so painful they will be welcomed back. That's optimism for you.

Xmas can be a hassle: If your children are married, they quarrel over which in-laws to invite and which to avoid; if you're alone you don't want to spend it by yourself, but nor do you want to burden a friend. If you can afford it, you could go to a hotel or on a cruise, which will be full of canoodling couples, though you might meet another solo senior. You could do something charitable like helping feed the homeless, or you could pull the covers over your head and wait until it passes. Season of goodwill and joy? Bah, humbug!

Yoga is something I admire but have never practiced. I like the idea of doing exercises that relax the mind, relieve stress, and keep the body trim, and those who go in for it look great and are infuriatingly calm. Of course we would all benefit from it, if we had the time. I'm going to save it for my old age.

Youth deserves our respect and sympathy. Think what we were like when we were their age, recall how little we've learned, and reflect on how much more difficult it is for them than it was for us, financially, politically, and emotionally. Remember what we admired about people who are now our age—their humor, generosity, individuality, courage, and ability to listen. Even if you don't have all of those qualities, you can still be nice to the young. They might even be nice in return.

Z

Zealots should be avoided at any age, especially if they're our contemporaries. Who needs people who lecture without listening, parade their prejudices with pride, and believe anyone who doesn't agree with them is not only wrong, but evil? It's bad enough when we come across a contemporary who has developed the missionary zeal of a convert, but it's even sadder and more dangerous when it's someone younger who might actually practice what they're preaching. Of course we must try to engage them in dialogue and get them to see reason, but with the true zealot it's a waste of breath and brain cells, unless it's your child that is involved.

We can hope that there will be enough people of sense to neutralize the effects of zealotry, but that's a pious hope at best.

The **Zeitgeist,** or spirit of the age, is slippery and multifaceted and no one knows how, why, or when it will change its shape or character. We have to pay it heed but we don't have to cave in to it. Of course we pride ourselves on our independent way of thinking and ascribe our successes to being different and standing out from the crowd. We shouldn't censor ourselves, but we've surely learned the hard way that timing is as important as talent (and perseverance) in any creative endeavor, and if you're not attuned to the zeitgeist, and can't subtly adapt to its shifting codes and strictures, you risk being caught up in the crowd of its victims, and unable to persuade anyone to listen to your defense.

Zoos are a problem: a great place to take our grandchildren, but what's our moral take on keeping wild animals in cages or enclosures? There are some zoos where the animals are kept in disgraceful conditions, but of the best we can say they are places to keep rare beasts from dying out or being poached or killed, where they can breed in safety and be properly looked after with, perhaps, a view to releasing some of their progeny back into the wild. We can show our grandchildren real live animals they might only see on television, even if they traveled to their native countries, and give them the experience of touching, smelling, and learning something about them. And yet, when we took our own grandchildren to a wildlife park we came across a giant anteater, walking around and around his enclosure, obviously stressed and bored and, for all we knew, lonely and sad. We'll never know if he'd be happier in the wild, but he certainly didn't look happy imprisoned in his exercise yard. With all our experience, it's not an easy thing to explain. But then, if you've read this far, you'll know that not every question has a straightforward answer.

About the Author

Peter Buckman has written books, plays, and scripts for film, television, and radio. He has been involved in the publishing industry for many years on both sides of the Atlantic, and he set up his own literary agency when he was in his sixties. *Still With It!* is his eighth book.